MEL BAY'S
DULCIMER CHORD ENCYCLOPEDIA

The first chord book in standard tunings for the Mountain Dulcimer!
Thousands of Chords, in 6 popular modes, 3 different tunings each!

By James Major

I would like to thank Laura Line Reep, Lisa Brashear, Gary Packard, Terri Major, Eric Hanada, and the whole Major family for their assistance in the making of this book.

Thank You

TABLE OF CONTENTS

THE AUTHOR
JAMES MAJOR

Jim was born and raised in the Detroit area. He started playing guitar in 1967 and bought his first dulcimer in 1970. Jim moved to Utah in 1972 and opened the Salt Lake Folk Music Center/Acoustic Music in 1974. Jim has sponsored the Storm Mountain Dulcimer Picnic annually since the late 70's. For more information write: Acoustic Music, 857 East 400, South, S.L.C., Utah 84102.

A NOTE ON DULCIMER CHORDS

Some of the chords in this book have a Doubled Root, 3rd, or 5th. Being limited to 3 strings on a Mountain Dulcimer (and with some chords requiring 4 or more notes) some of the chords are considered incomplete.

HOW TO READ THE CHORD DIAGRAMS

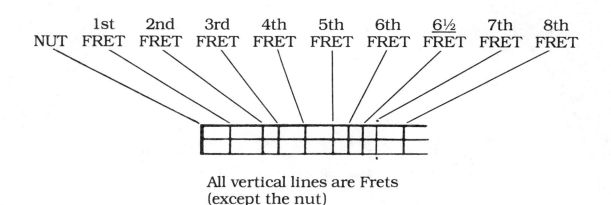

1st 2nd 3rd 4th 5th 6th 6½ 7th 8th
NUT FRET FRET FRET FRET FRET FRET FRET FRET FRET

All vertical lines are Frets
(except the nut)

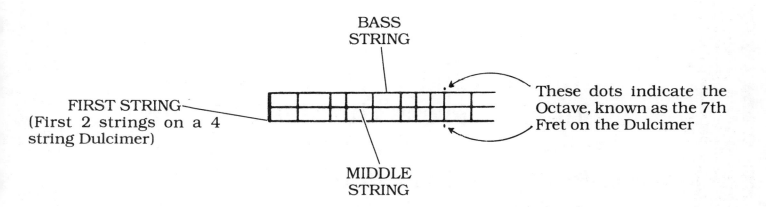

BASS
STRING

FIRST STRING
(First 2 strings on a 4
string Dulcimer)

MIDDLE
STRING

These dots indicate the
Octave, known as the 7th
Fret on the Dulcimer

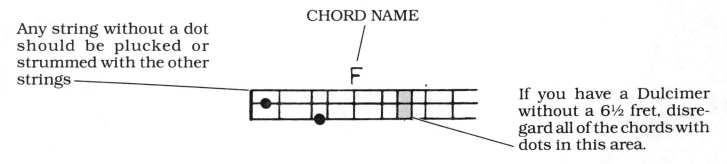

CHORD NAME

F

Any string without a dot
should be plucked or
strummed with the other
strings

If you have a Dulcimer
without a 6½ fret, disre-
gard all of the chords with
dots in this area.

Dots represent where you
press the strings down
with your fingers

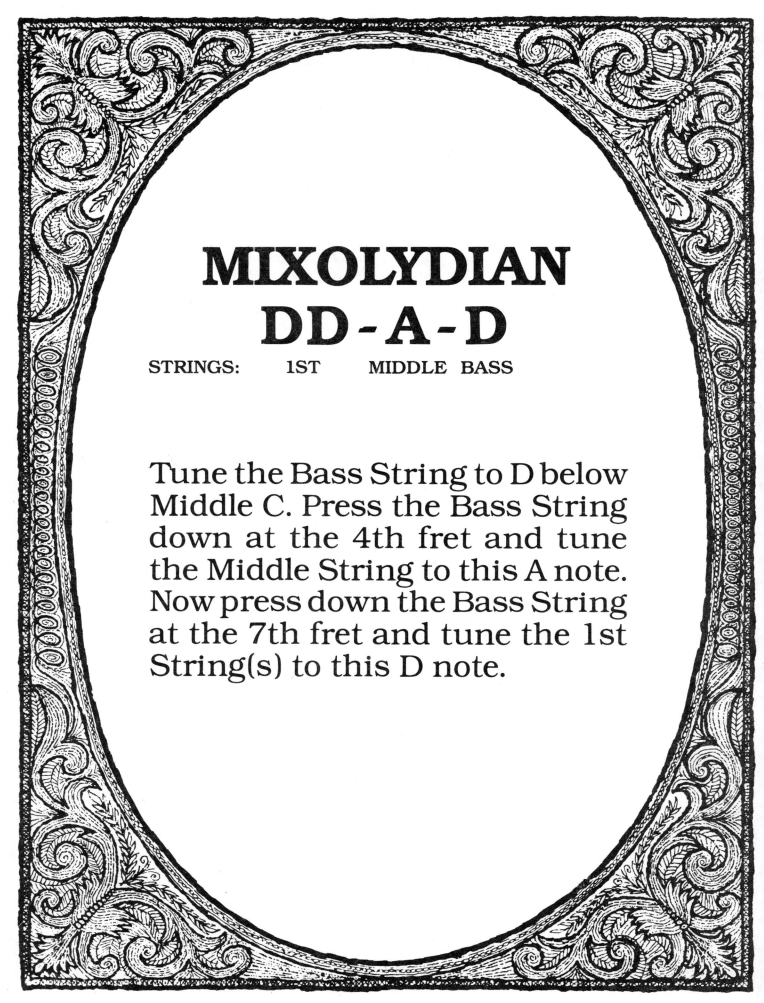

MIXOLYDIAN
DD - A - D

STRINGS: 1ST MIDDLE BASS

Tune the Bass String to D below Middle C. Press the Bass String down at the 4th fret and tune the Middle String to this A note. Now press down the Bass String at the 7th fret and tune the 1st String(s) to this D note.

MIXOLYDIAN DD-A-D

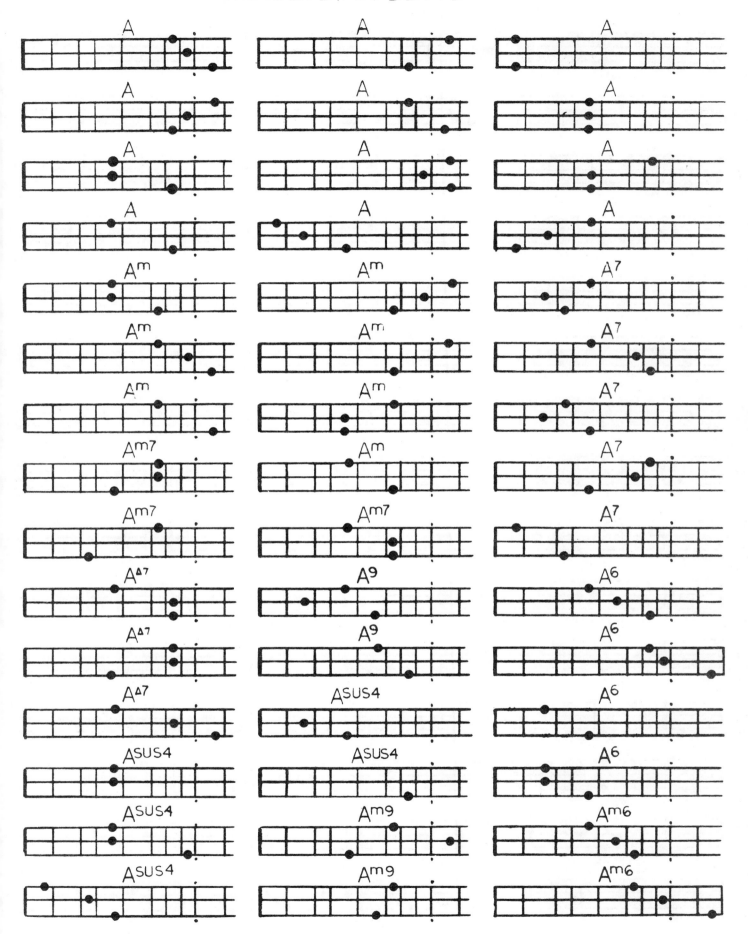

MIXOLYDIAN DD-A-D

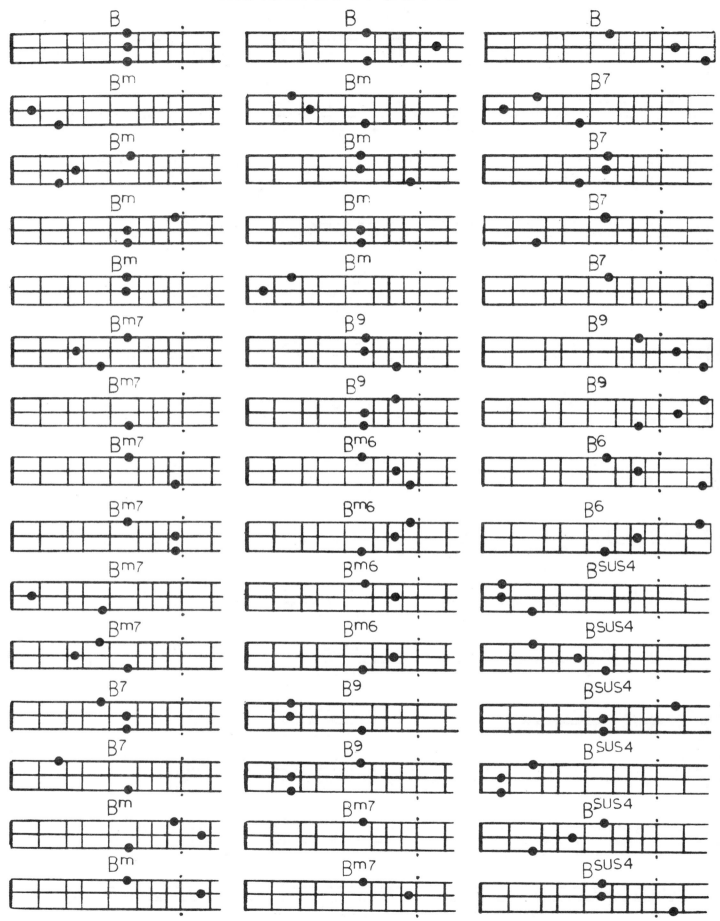

MIXOLYDIAN DD-A-D

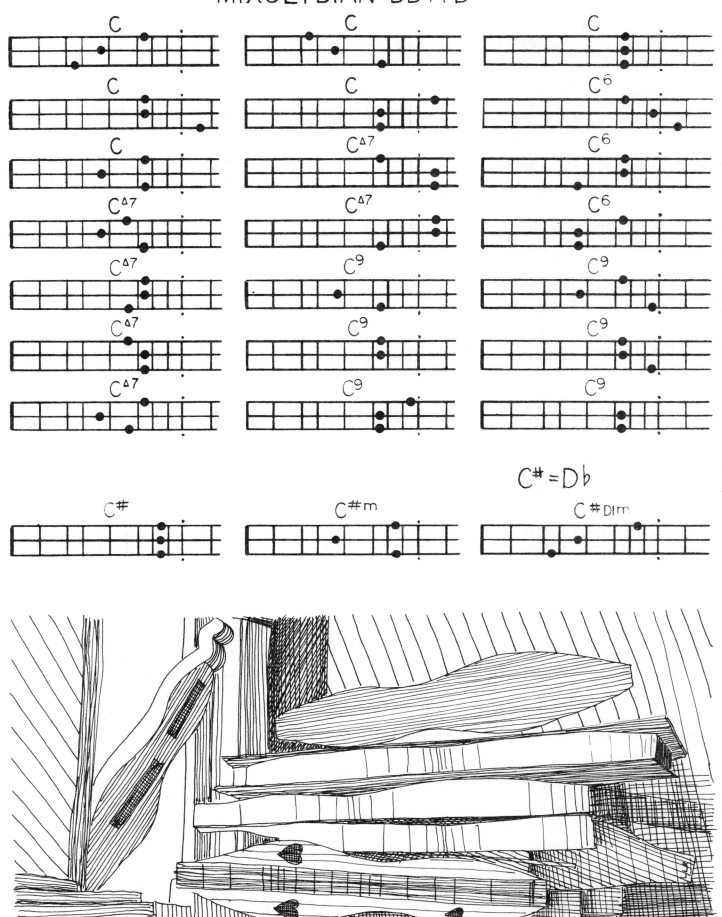

MIXOLYDIAN DD-A-D

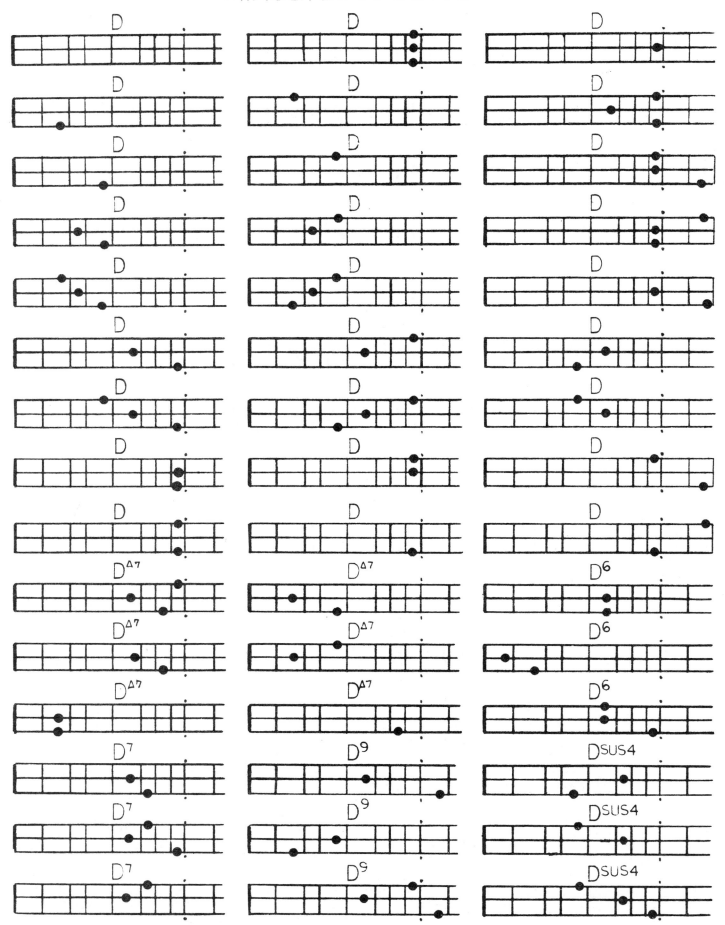

MIXOLYDIAN DD-A-D

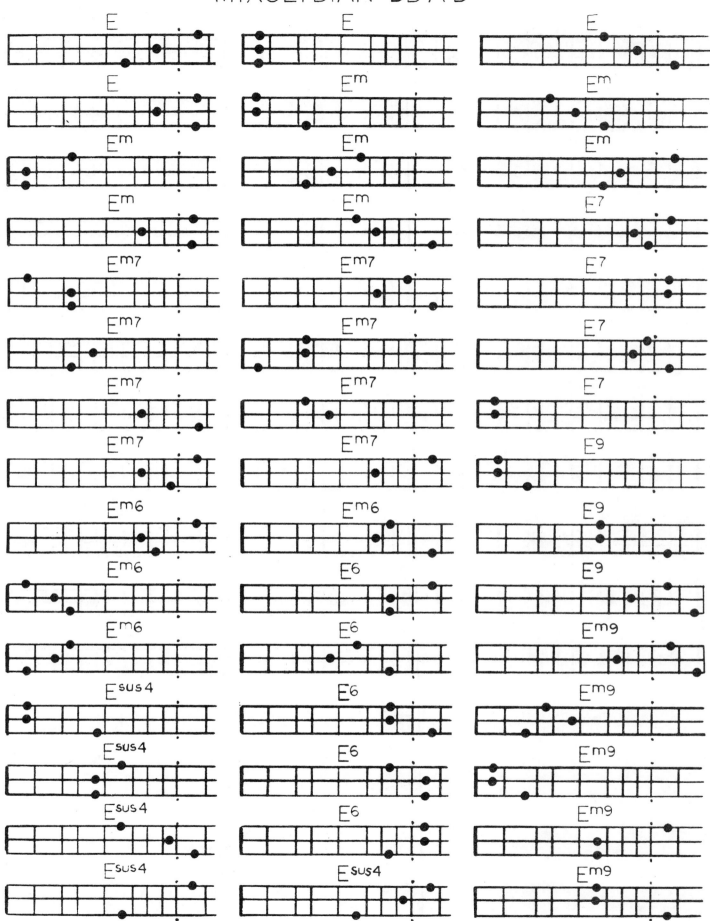

MIXOLYDIAN DD-A-D

F#=Gb

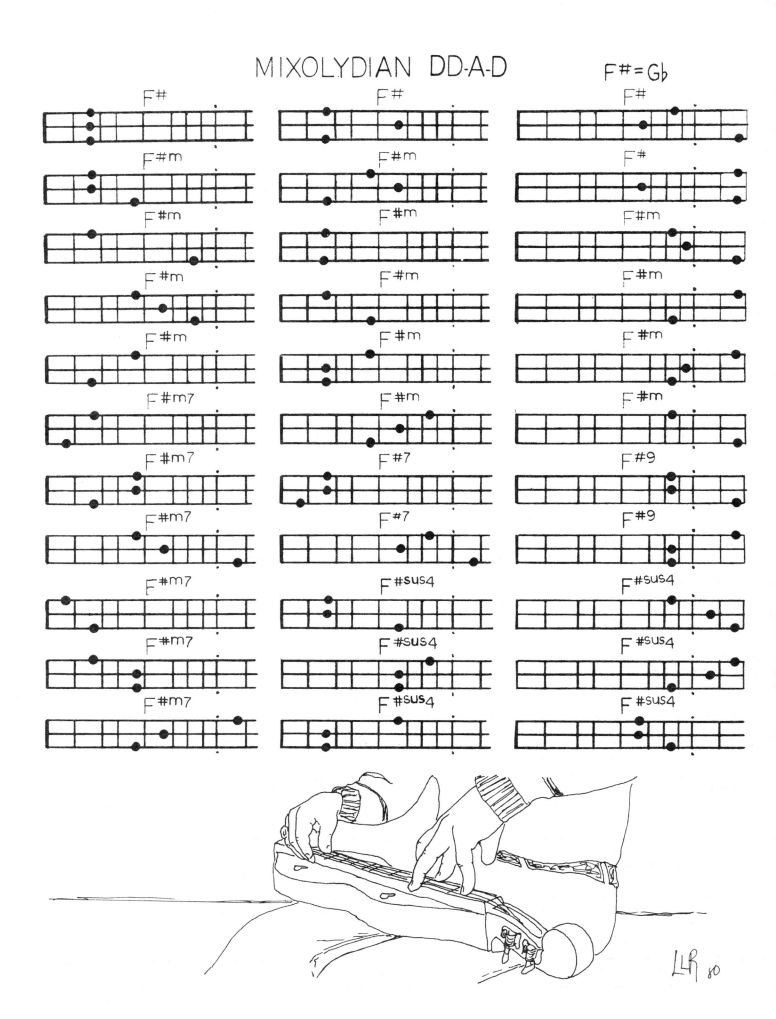

MIXOLYDIAN DD-A-D

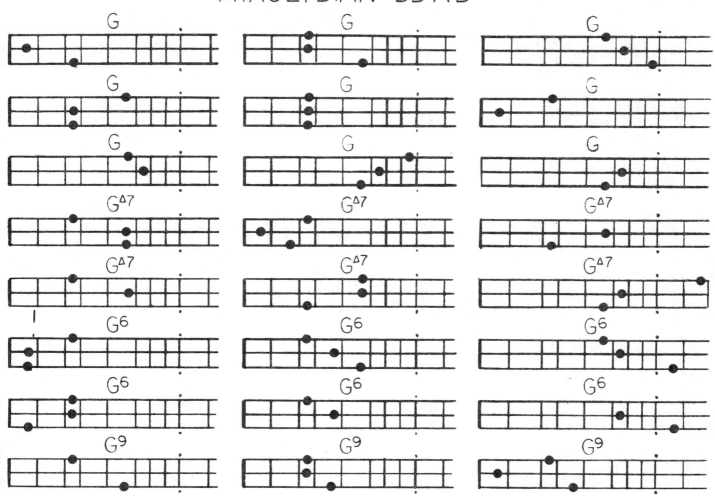

MIXOLYDIAN
GG - D - G

STRINGS: 1ST   MIDDLE   BASS

Tune the Bass String to G below Middle C. Press down the Bass String at the 4th fret and tune the Middle String to this D note. Now press down the Bass String at the 7th fret and tune the 1st String(s) to this G note.

MIXOLYDIAN GG-D-G

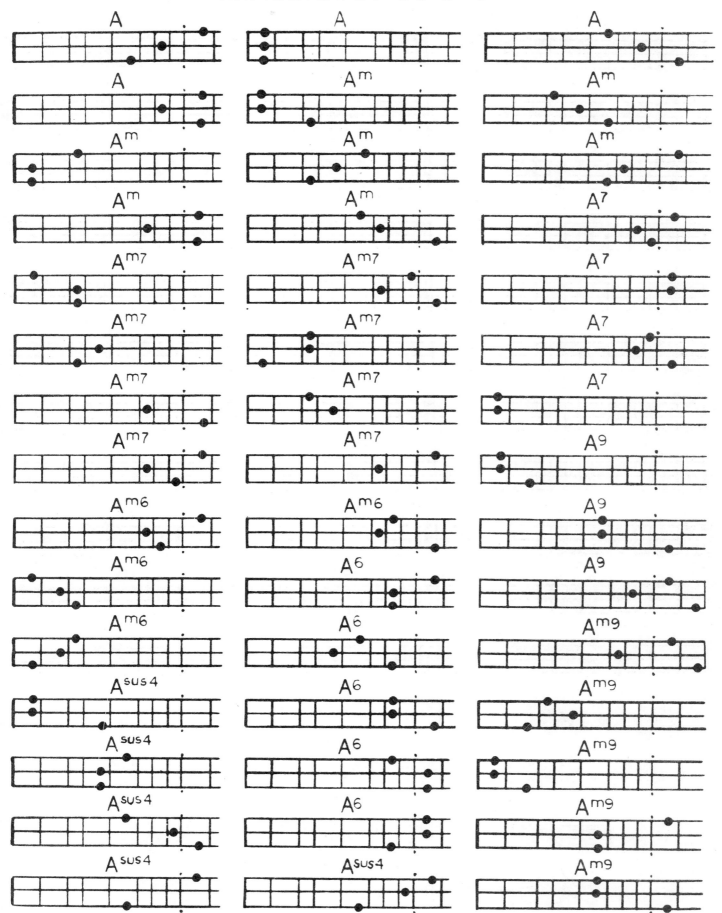

MIXOLYDIAN GG-D-G

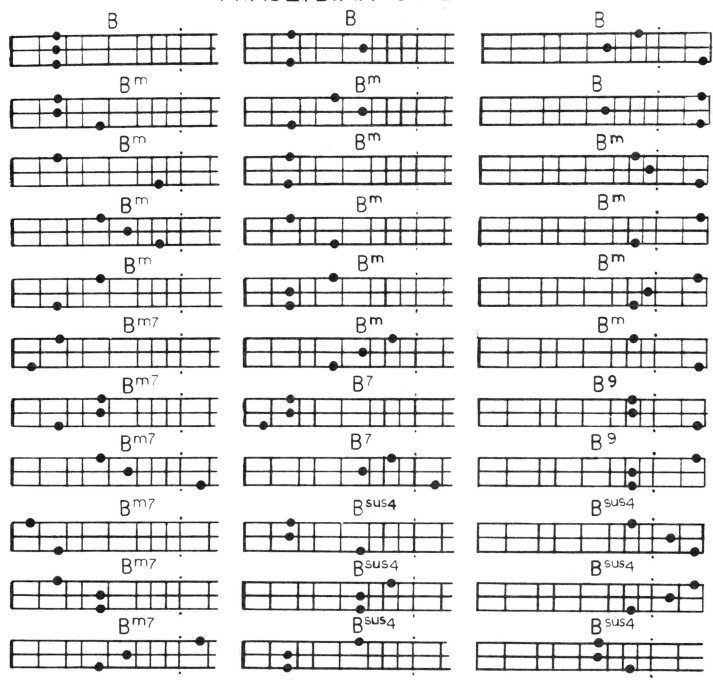

LLR 00

MIXOLYDIAN GG-D-G

MIXOLYDIAN GG-D-G

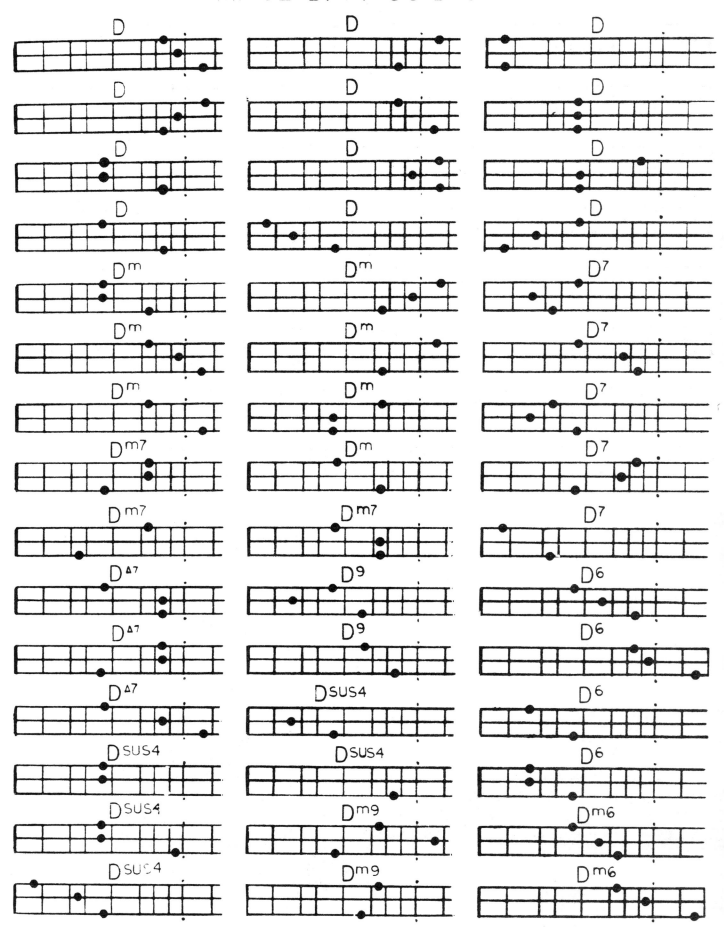

MIXOLYDIAN GG-D-G

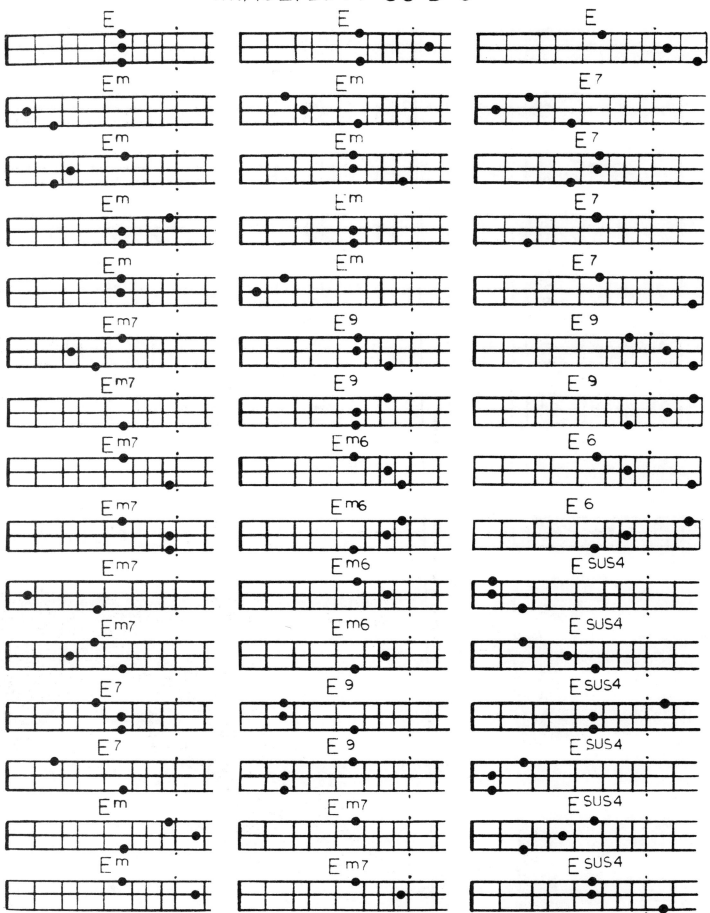

MIXOLYDIAN GG-D-G

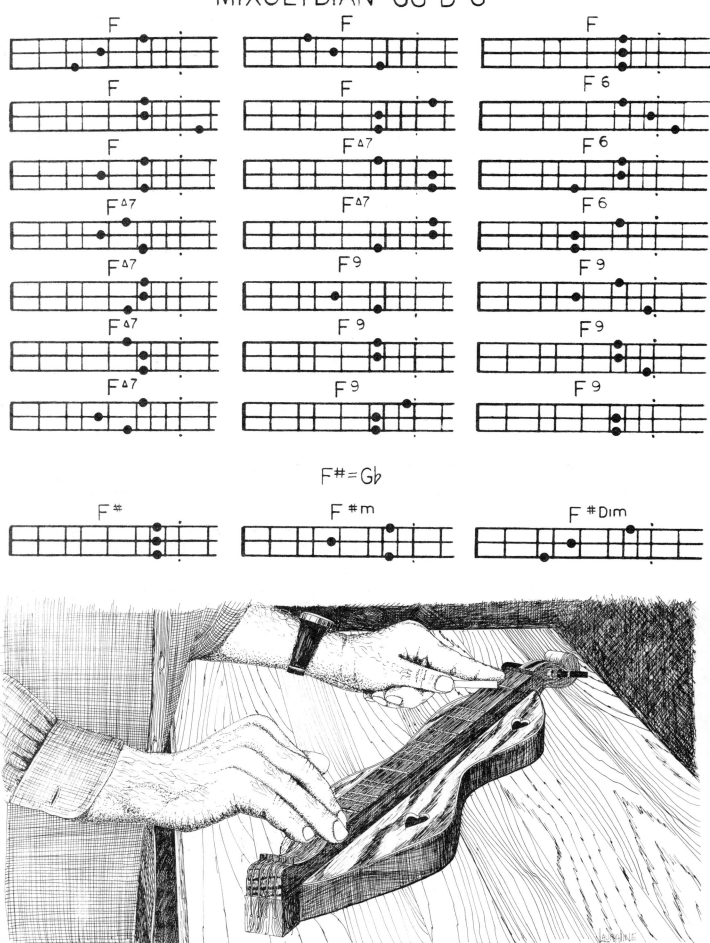

MIXOLYDIAN GG-D-G

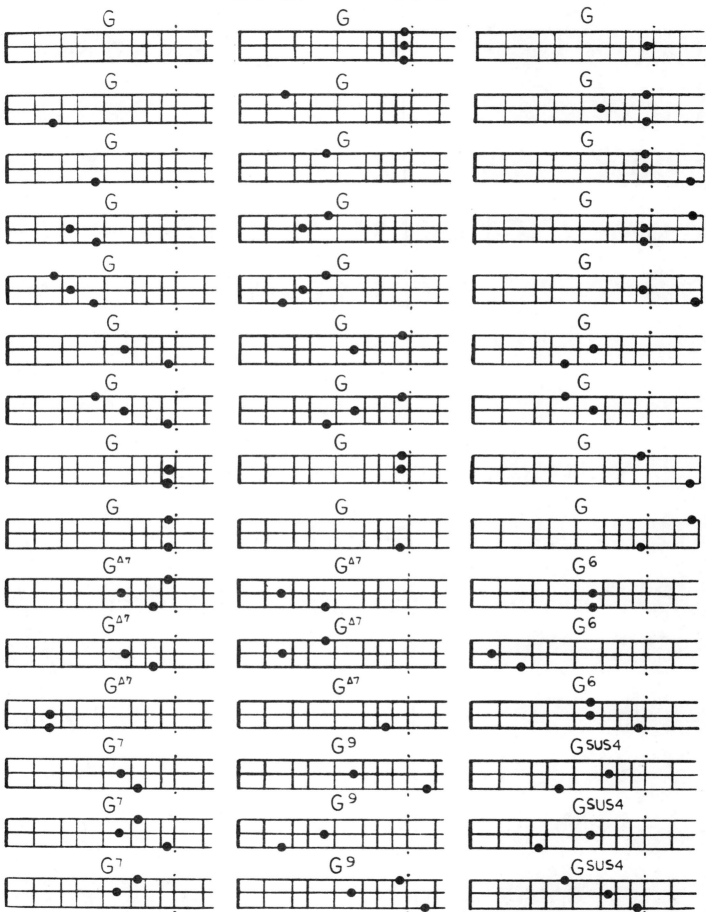

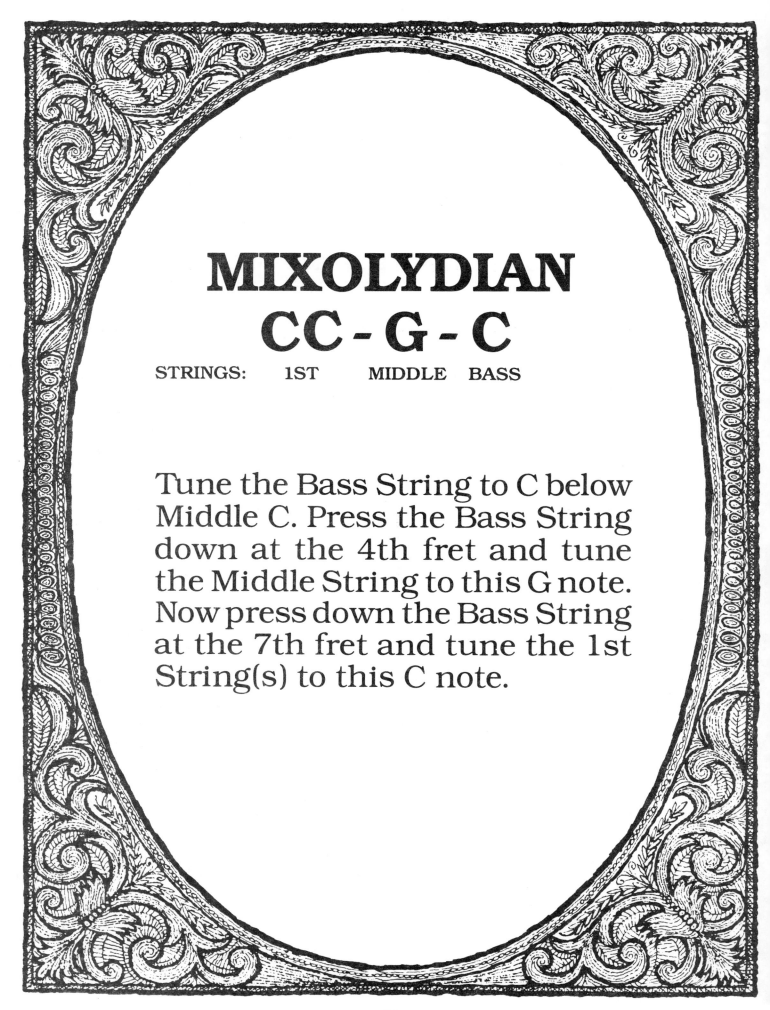

MIXOLYDIAN
CC - G - C

STRINGS: 1ST   MIDDLE   BASS

Tune the Bass String to C below Middle C. Press the Bass String down at the 4th fret and tune the Middle String to this G note. Now press down the Bass String at the 7th fret and tune the 1st String(s) to this C note.

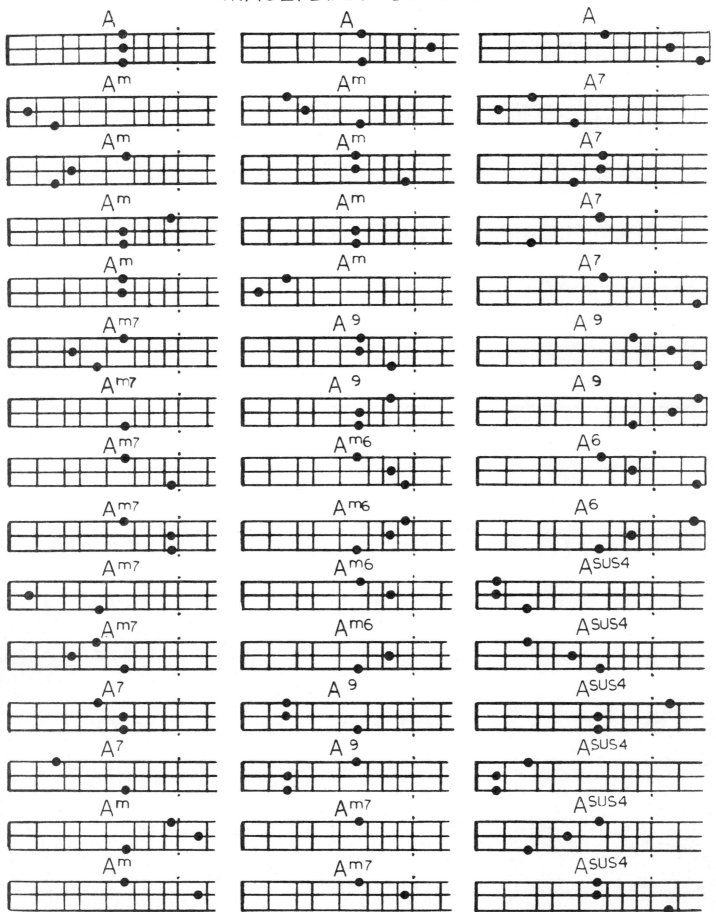

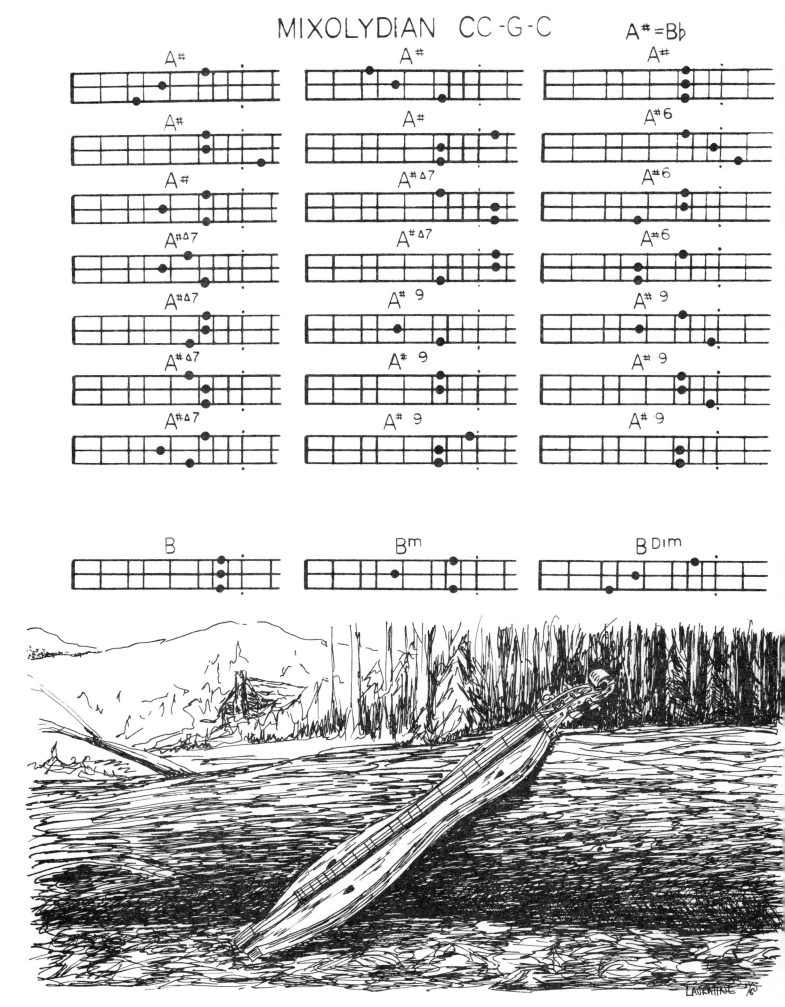

MIXOLYDIAN CC-G-C

A♯=B♭

MIXOLYDIAN CC-G-C

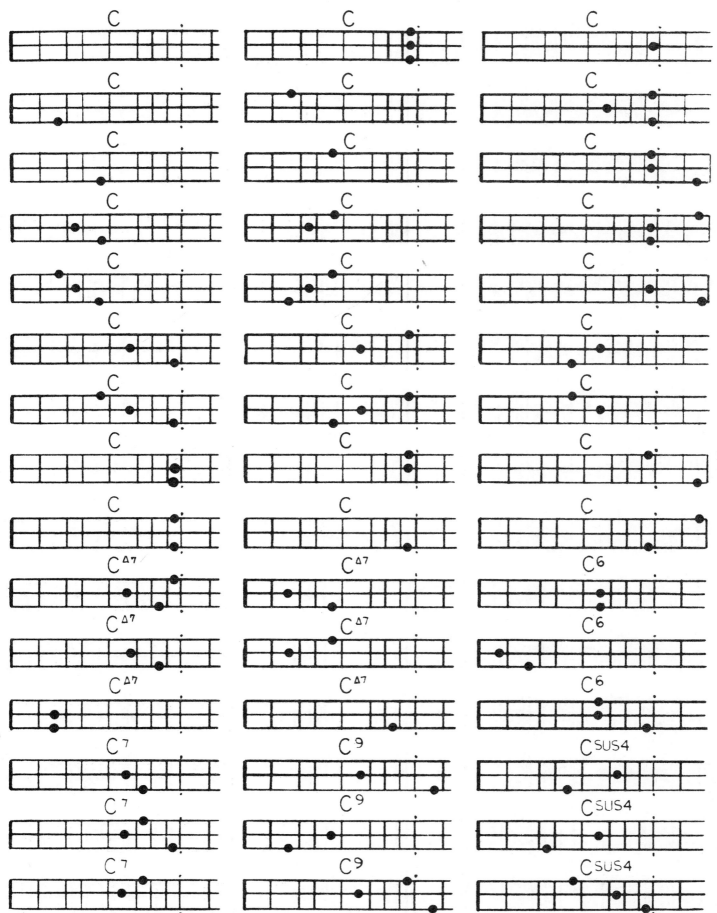

27

MIXOLYDIAN CC-G-C

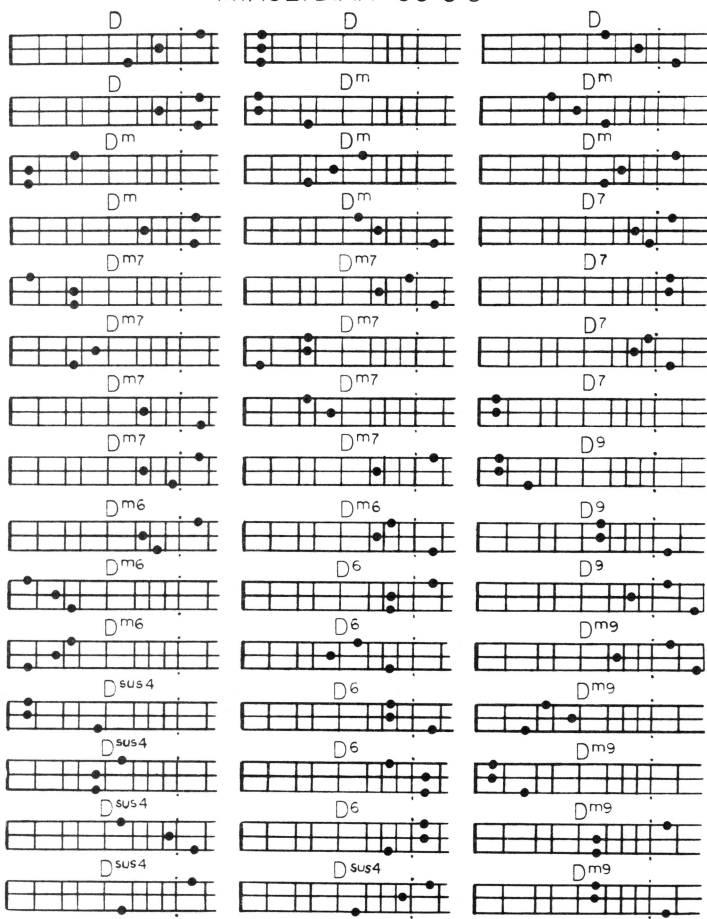

28

MIXOLYDIAN CC-G-C

MIXOLYDIAN CC-G-C

MIXOLYDIAN CC-G-C

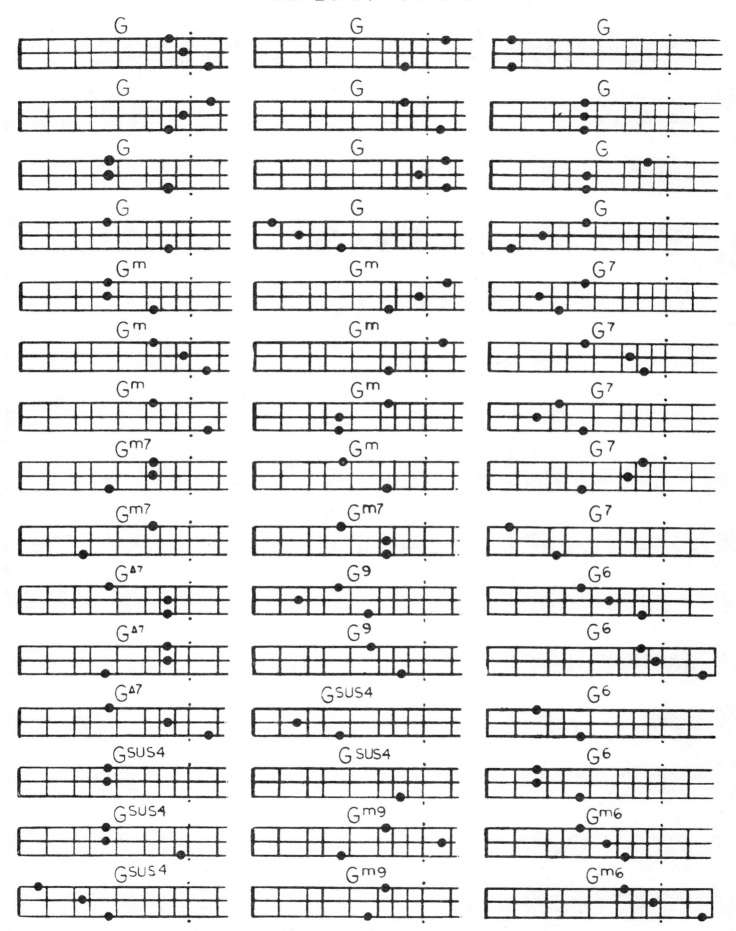

31

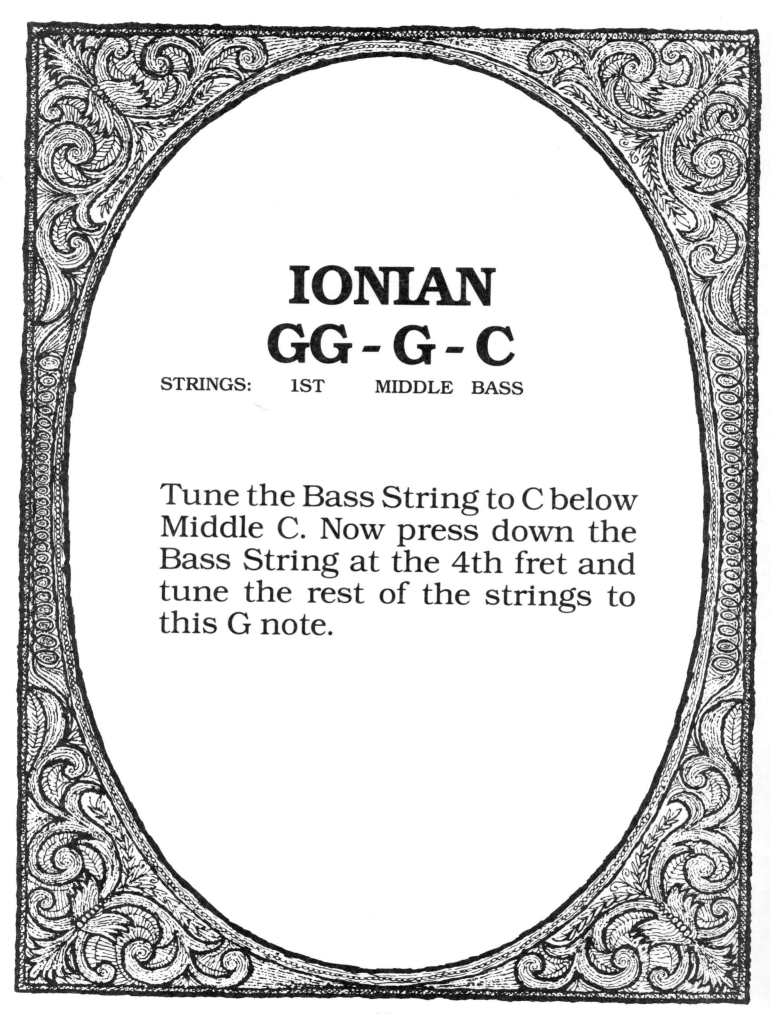

IONIAN
GG - G - C

STRINGS: 1ST   MIDDLE BASS

Tune the Bass String to C below Middle C. Now press down the Bass String at the 4th fret and tune the rest of the strings to this G note.

IONIAN GG-G-C

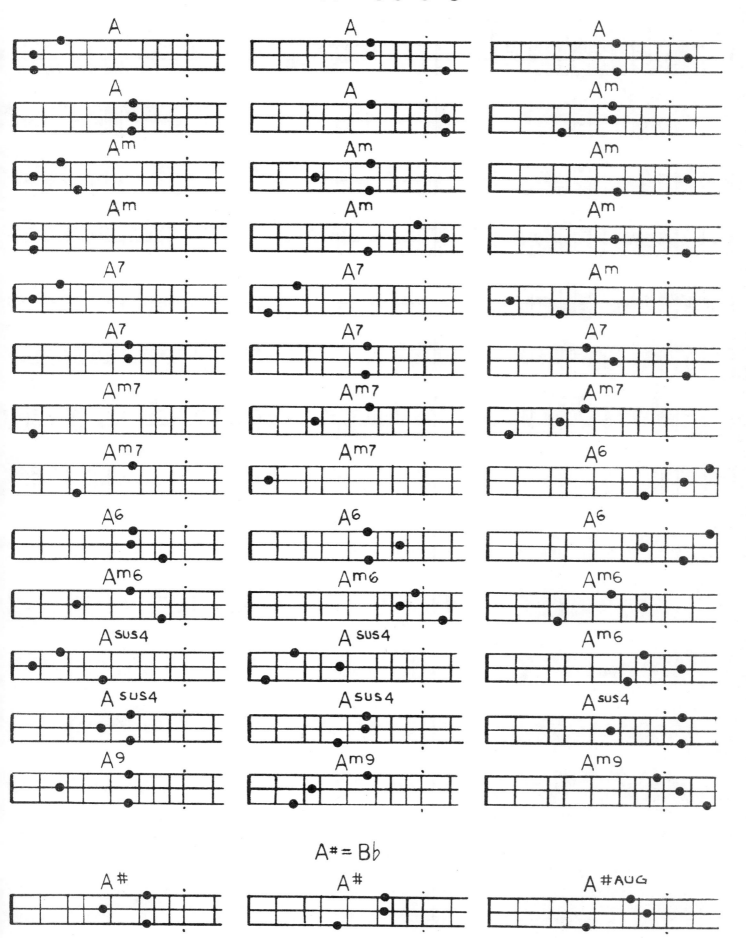

IONIAN   GG-G-C

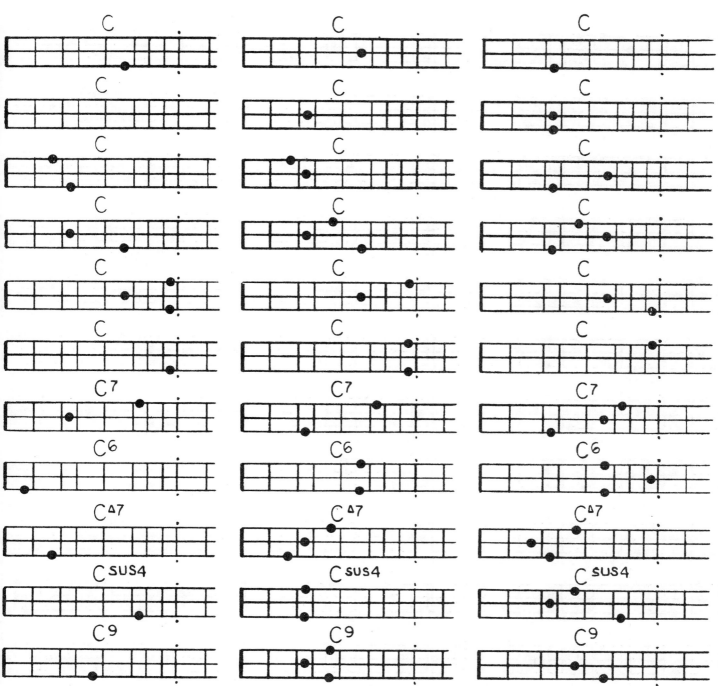

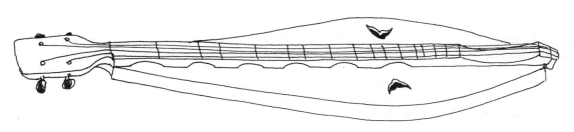

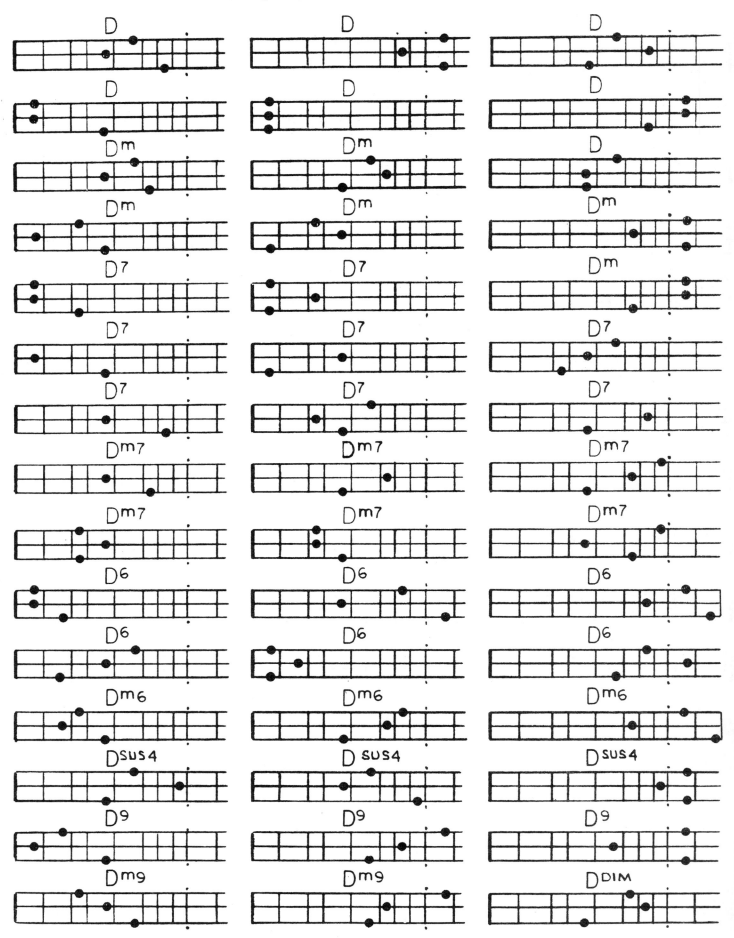

IONIAN GG-G-C

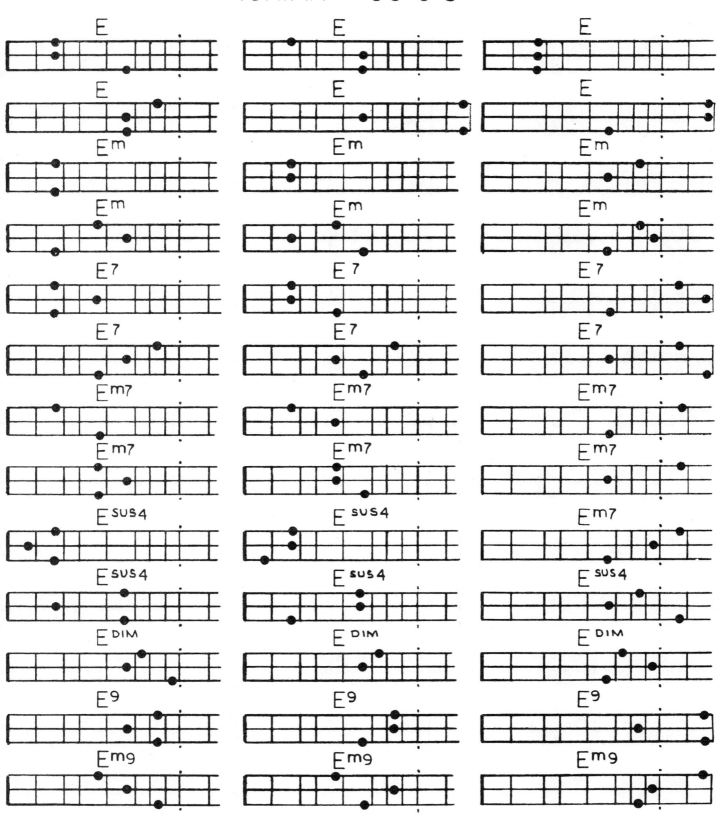

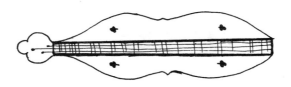

IONIAN GG-G-C

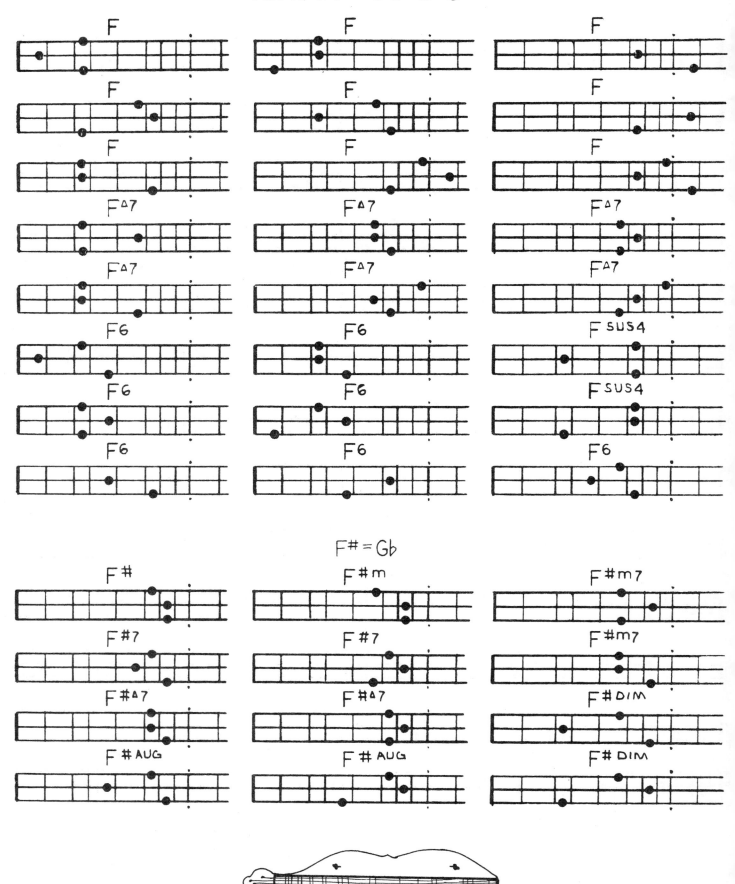

IONIAN GG-G-C

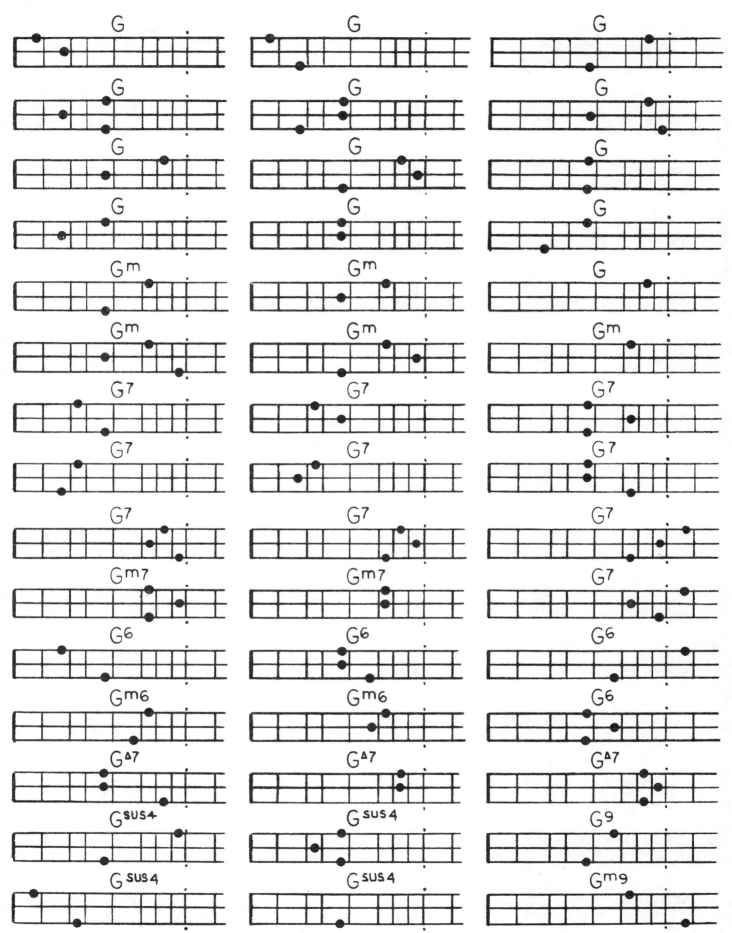

39

IONIAN
AA - A - D

STRINGS: 1ST   MIDDLE   BASS

Tune the Bass String to D below Middle C. Now press down the Bass String at the 4th fret and tune the rest of the strings to this A note.

IONIAN AA-A-D

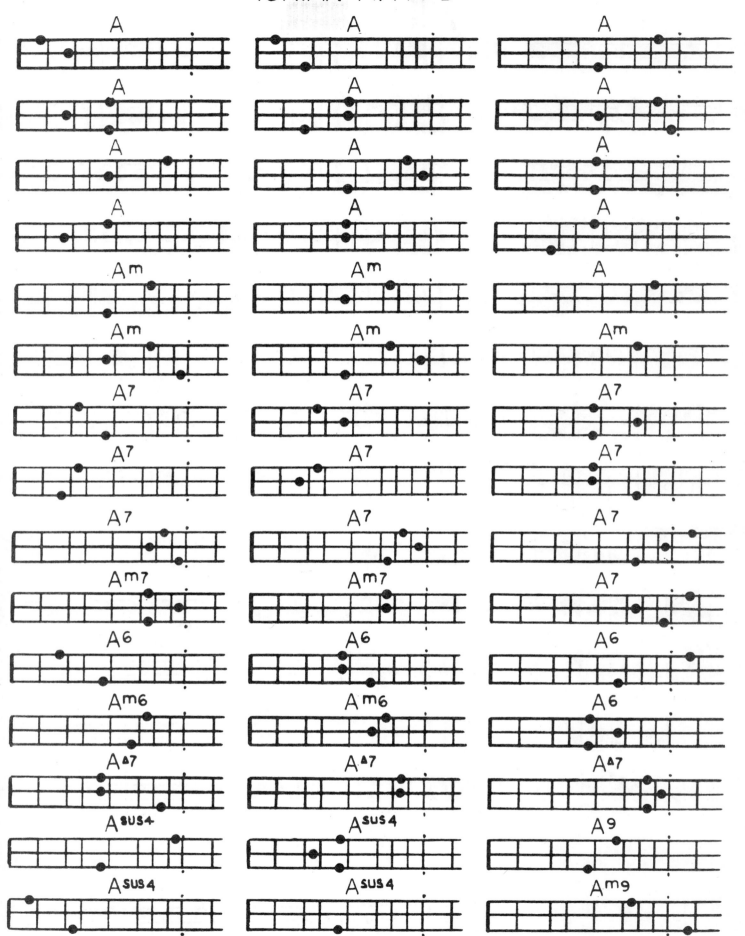

IONIAN AA-A-D

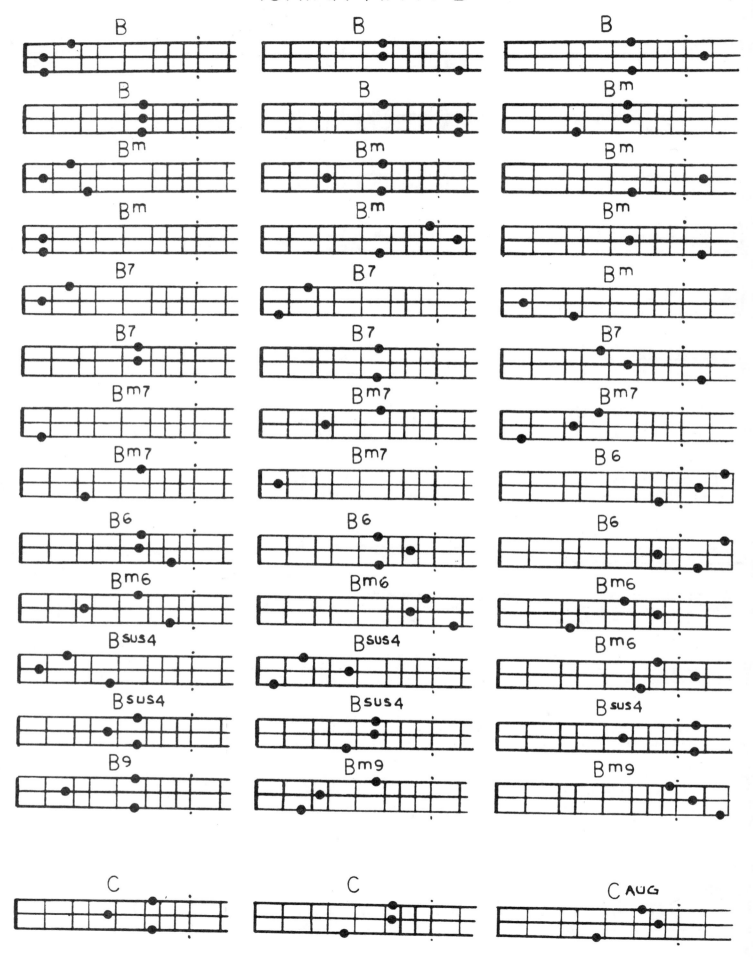

IONIAN AA-A-D

43

IONIAN AA-A-D

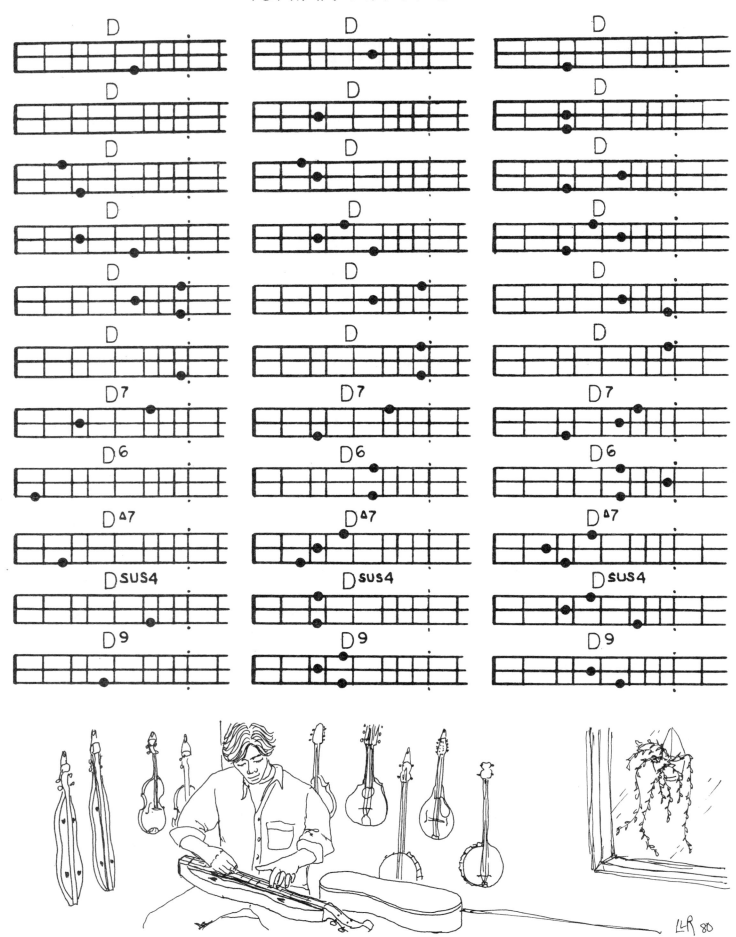

IONIAN AA-A-D

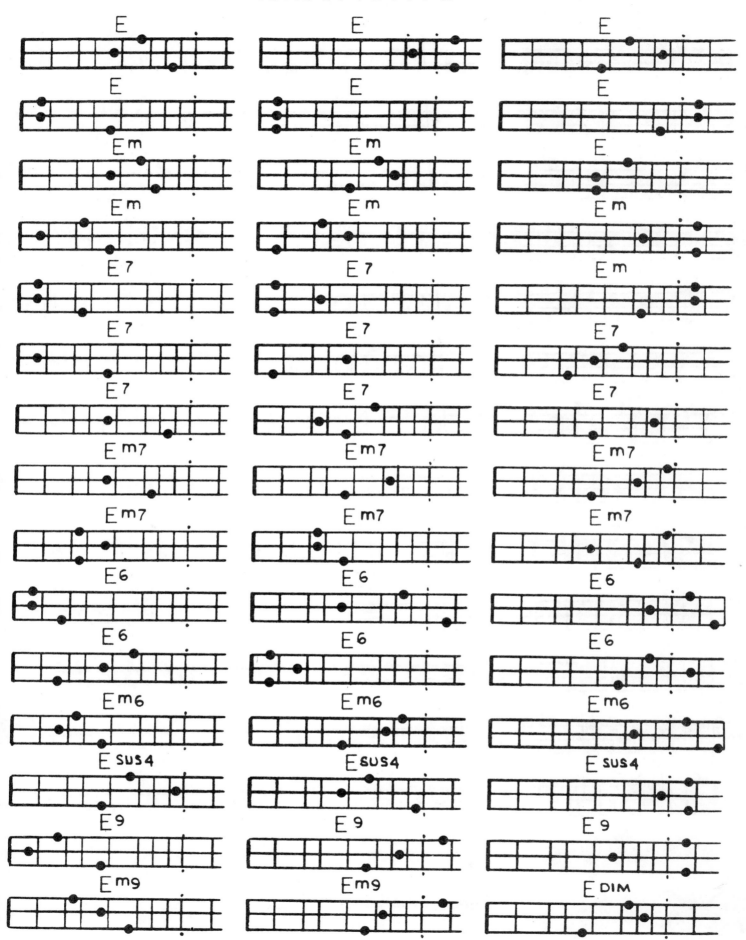

IONIAN AA-A-D

F♯=G♭

IONIAN AA-A-D

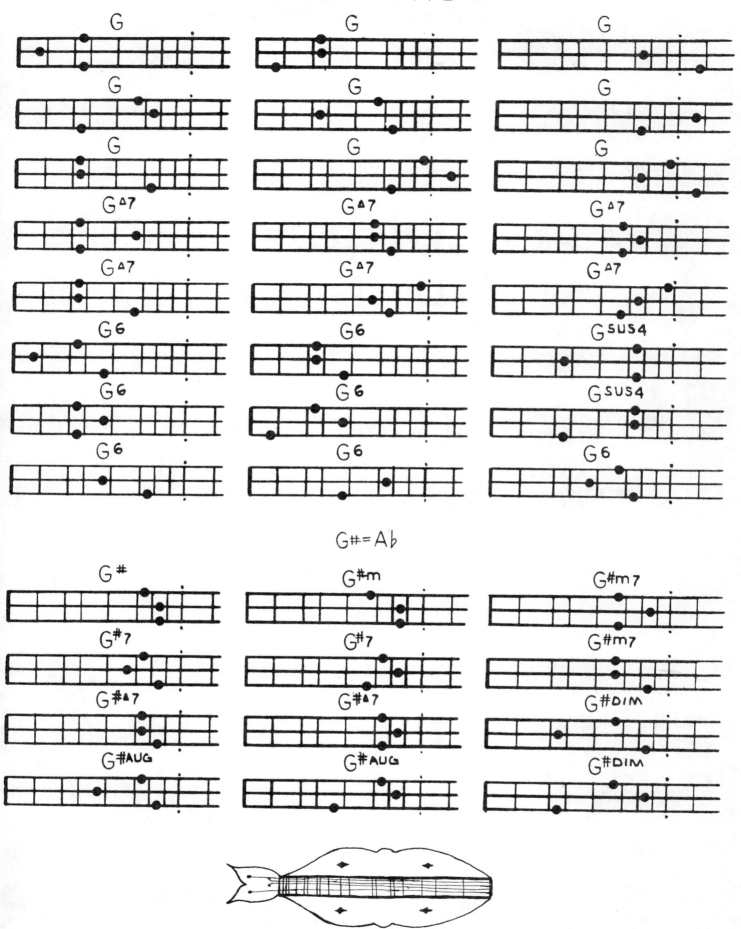

IONIAN
DD - D - G

STRINGS:　　　1ST　　　MIDDLE　　BASS

Tune the Bass String to G below Middle C. Now press down the Bass String at the 4th fret and tune the rest of the strings to this D note.

IONIAN DD-D-G

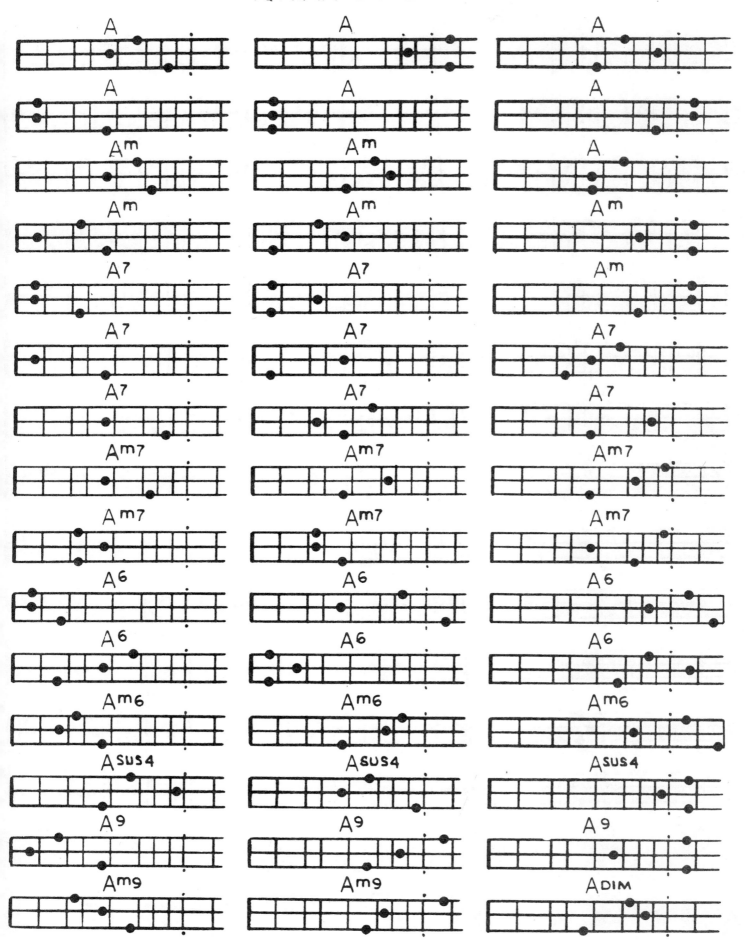

IONIAN DD - D - G

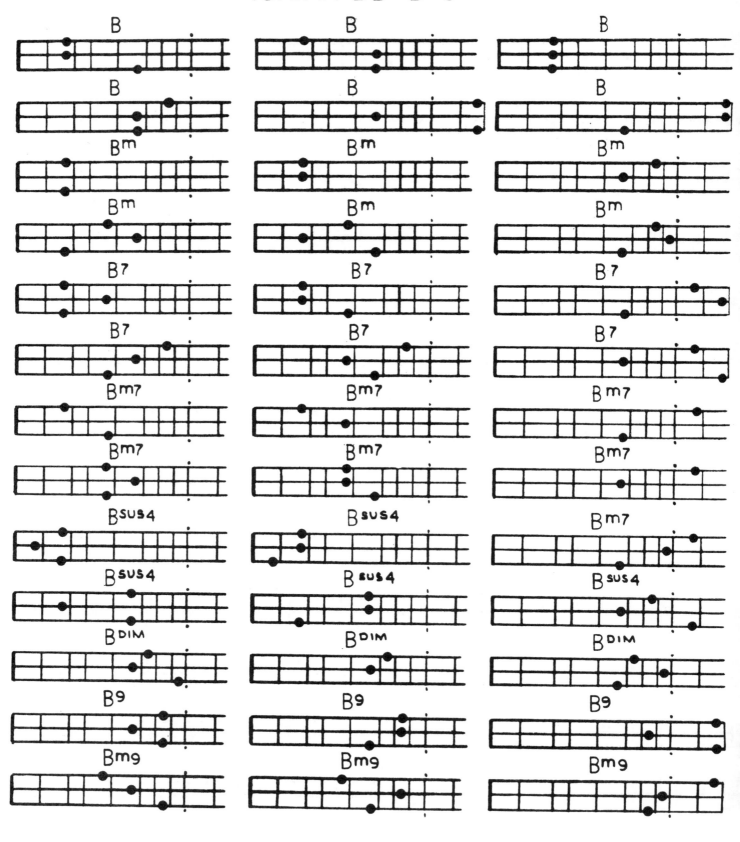

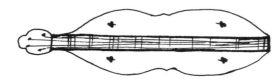

IONIAN DD-D-G

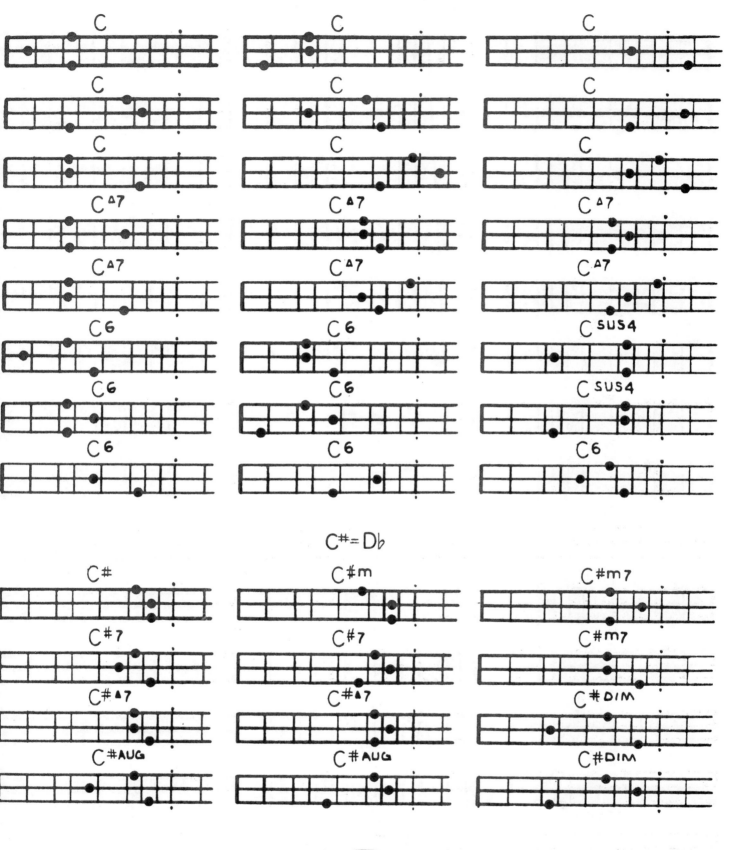

IONIAN DD-D-G

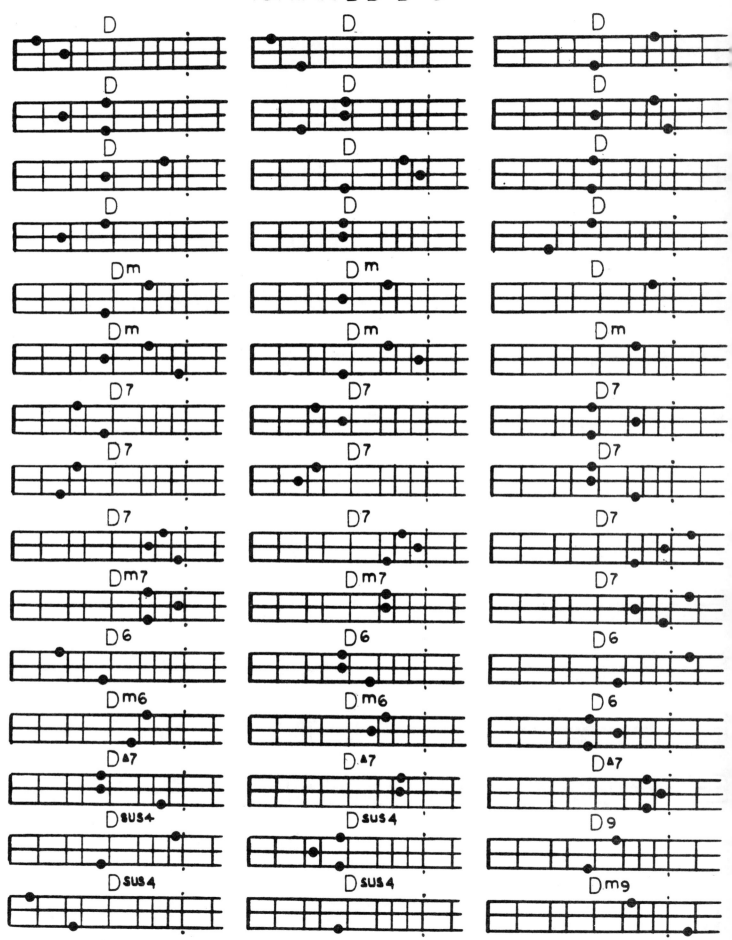

IONIAN DD-D-G

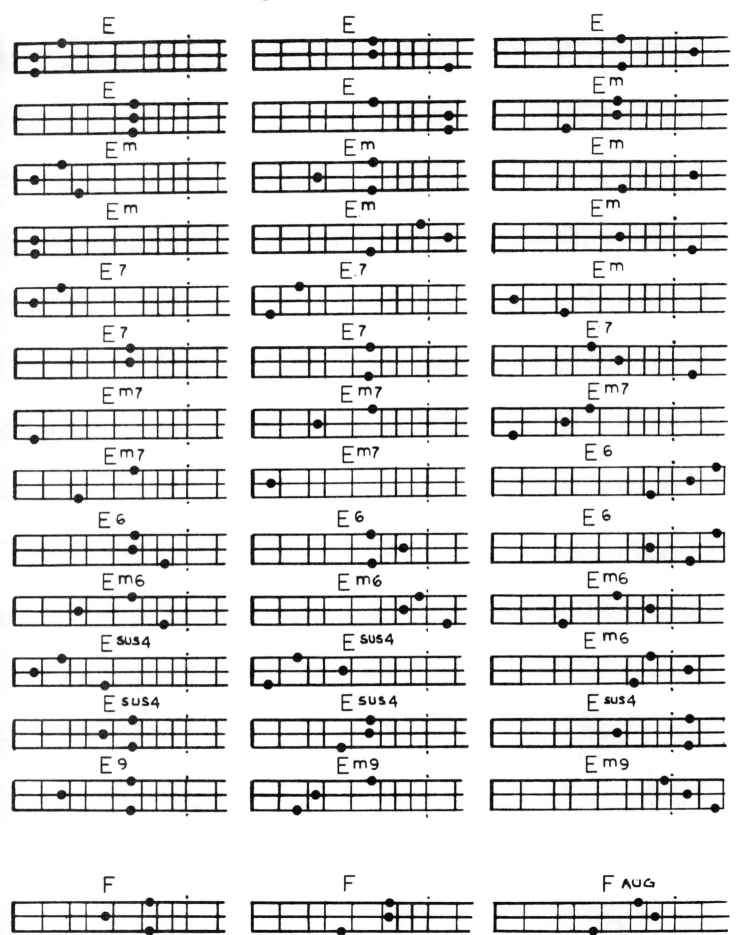

IONIAN DD - D = G

IONIAN DD-D-G

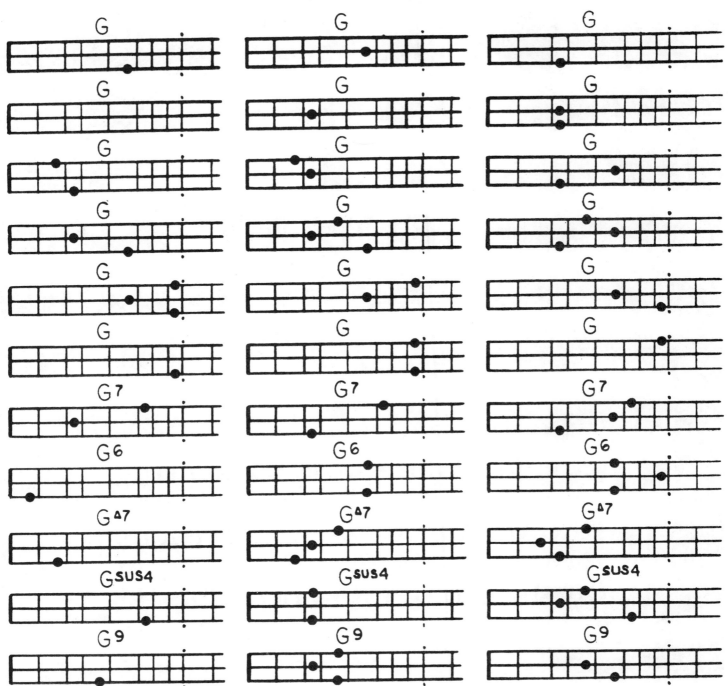

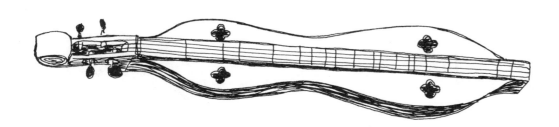

LLR 80

AEOLIAN
B♭ B♭ - G - C

STRING: 1ST   MIDDLE   BASS

Tune the Bass String to C below Middle C. Press the bass string down at the 4th fret and tune the Middle String to this G note. Now press the Bass String down at the 6th fret and tune the 1st String(s) to this B♭ note.

AEOLIAN B♭B♭-G-C

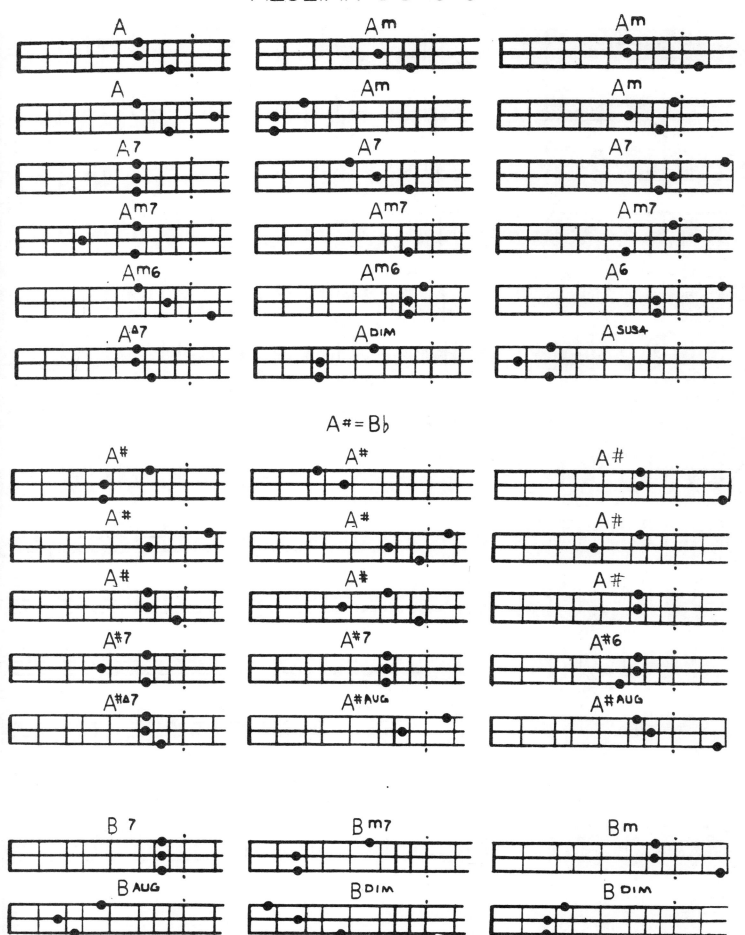

AEOLIAN B♭-B♭-G-C

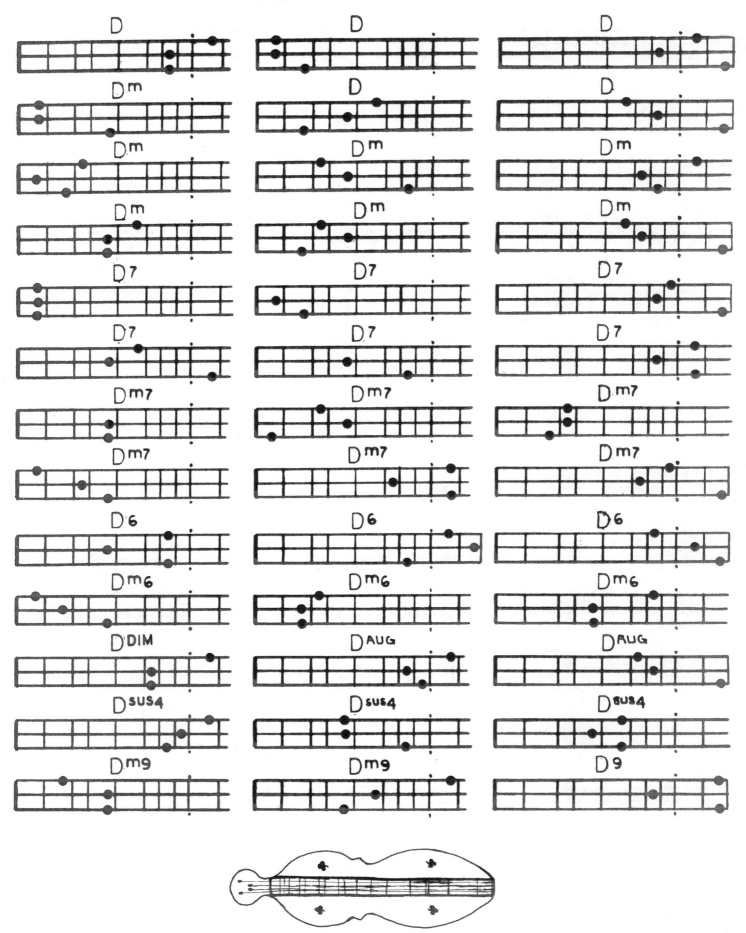

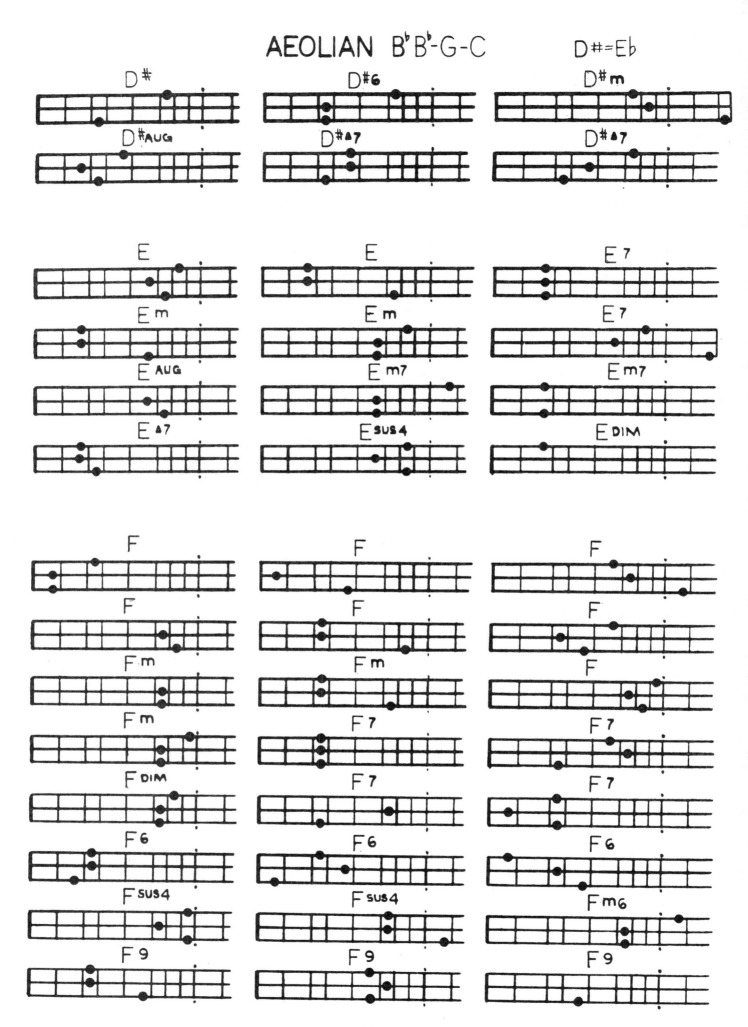

AEOLIAN B♭B♭-G-C

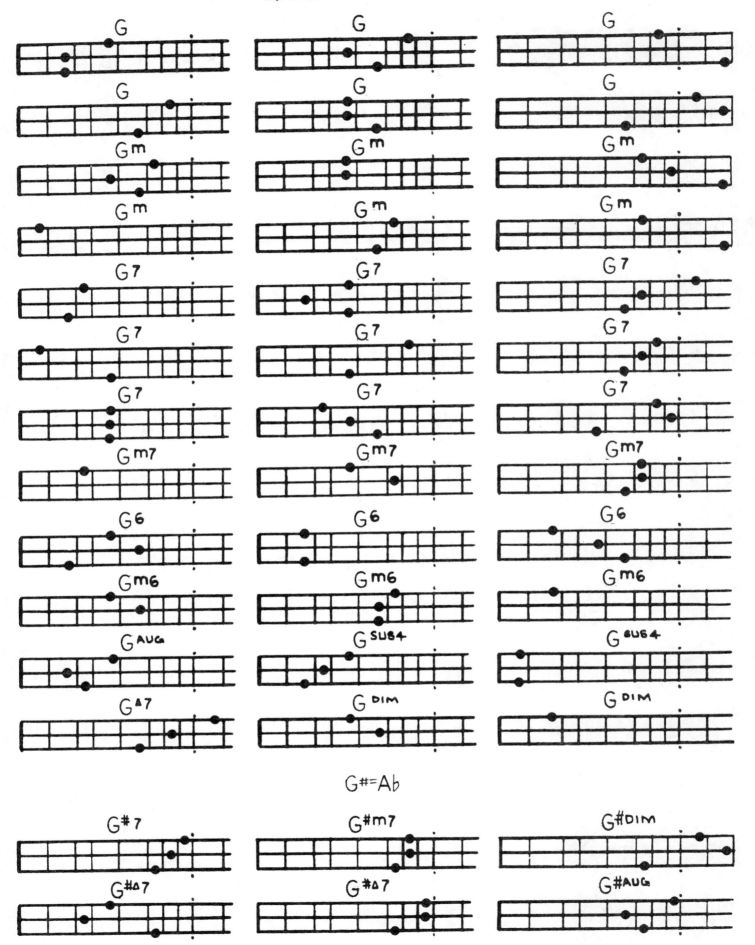

G#=A♭

61

AEOLIAN
CC - A - D

STRINGS: 1ST   MIDDLE BASS

Tune the Bass String to D below Middle C. Press the Bass String down at the 4th fret and tune the Middle String to this A note. Now press the Bass String down at the 6th fret and tune the 1st String(s) to this C note.

AEOLIAN CC-A-D

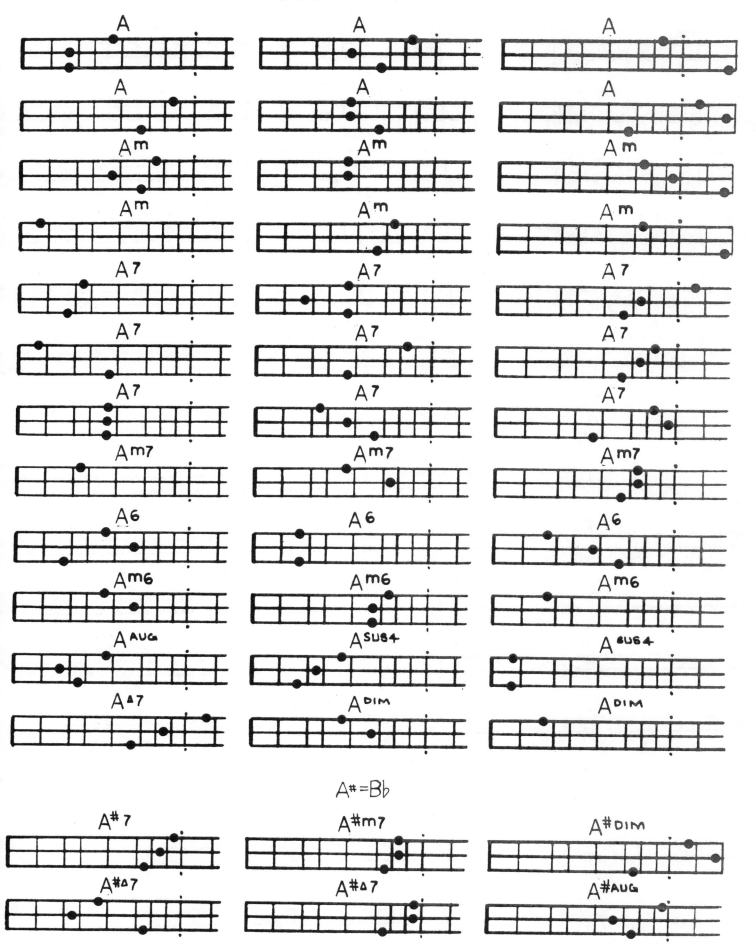

63

AEOLIAN CC-A-D

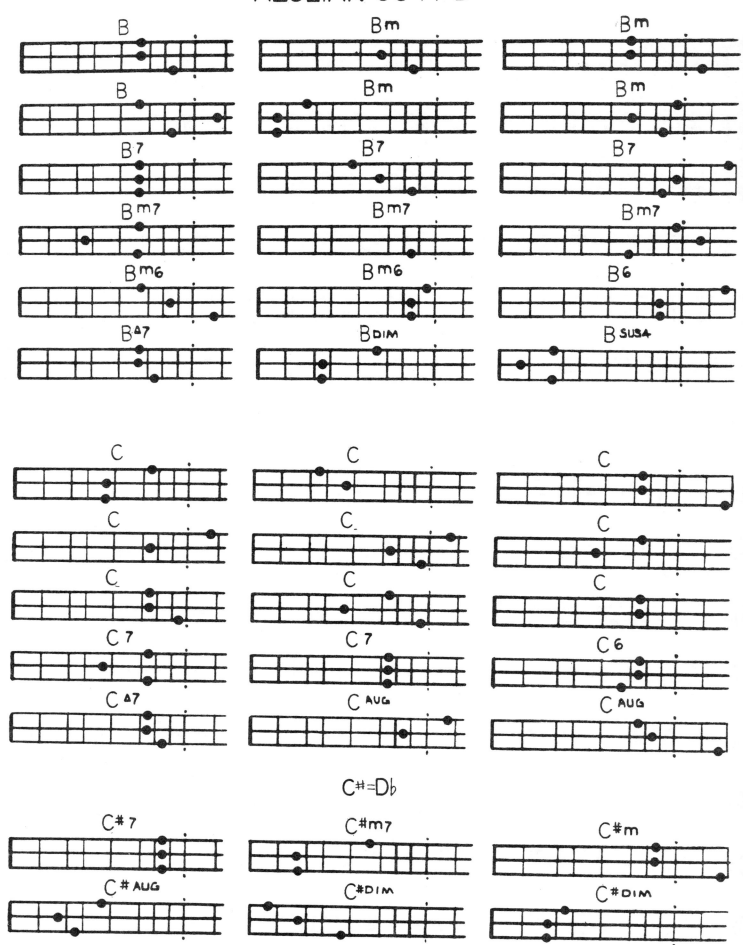

AEOLIAN CC-A-D

AEOLIAN CC-A-D

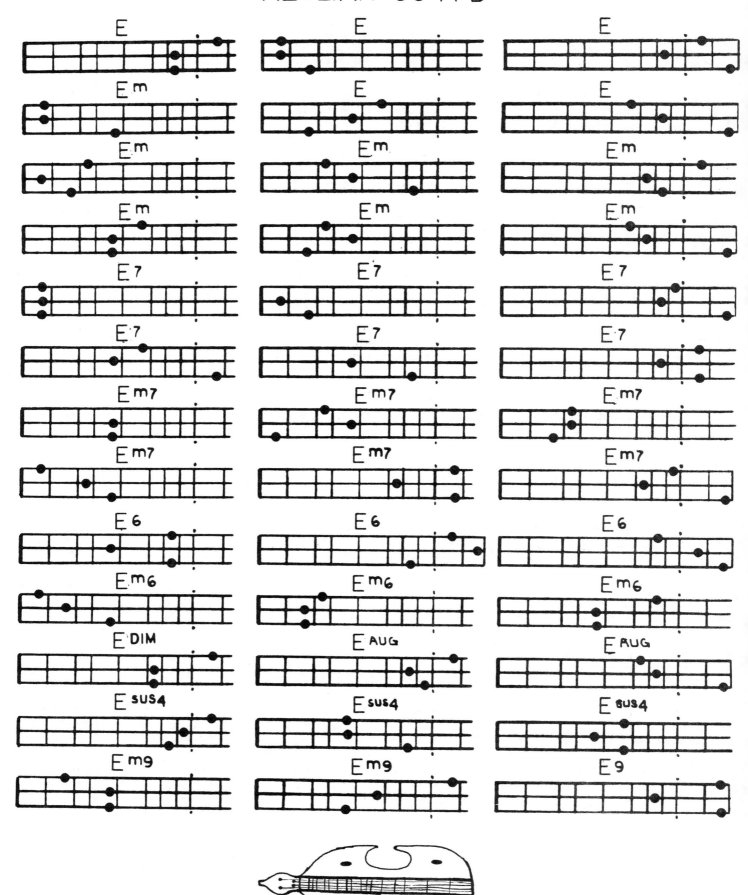

AEOLIAN CC-A-D

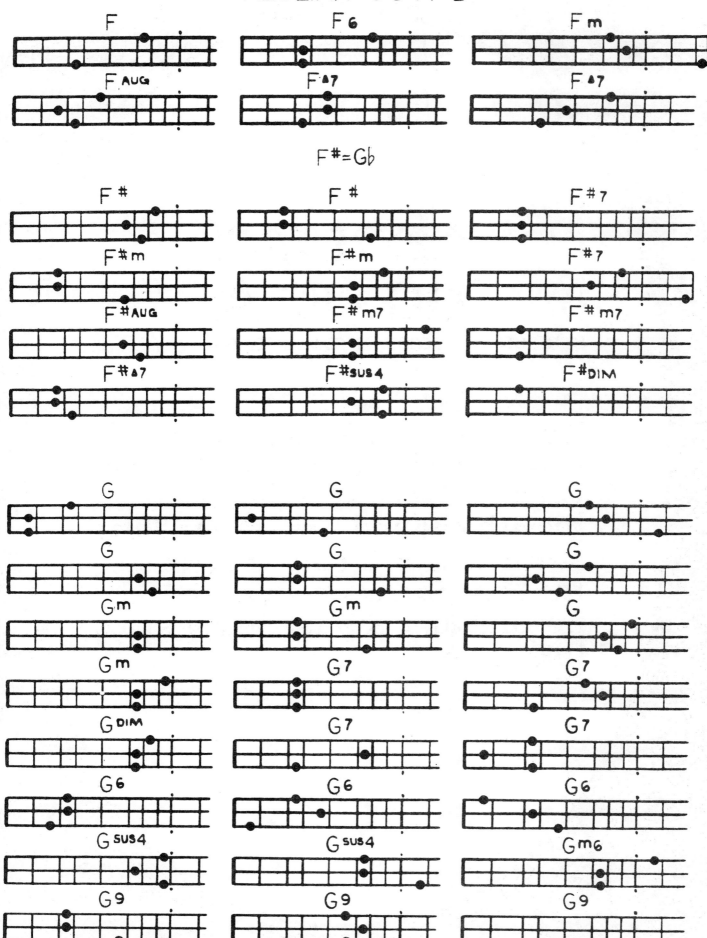

AEOLIAN
GG - E - A

STRINGS: 1ST   MIDDLE   BASS

Tune the Bass String to A an octave and 1½ steps below Middle C. Press the Bass String down at the 4th fret and tune the Middle string to this E note. Now press the Bass String down at the 6th fret and tune the 1st String(s) to this G note.

AEOLIAN GG-E-A

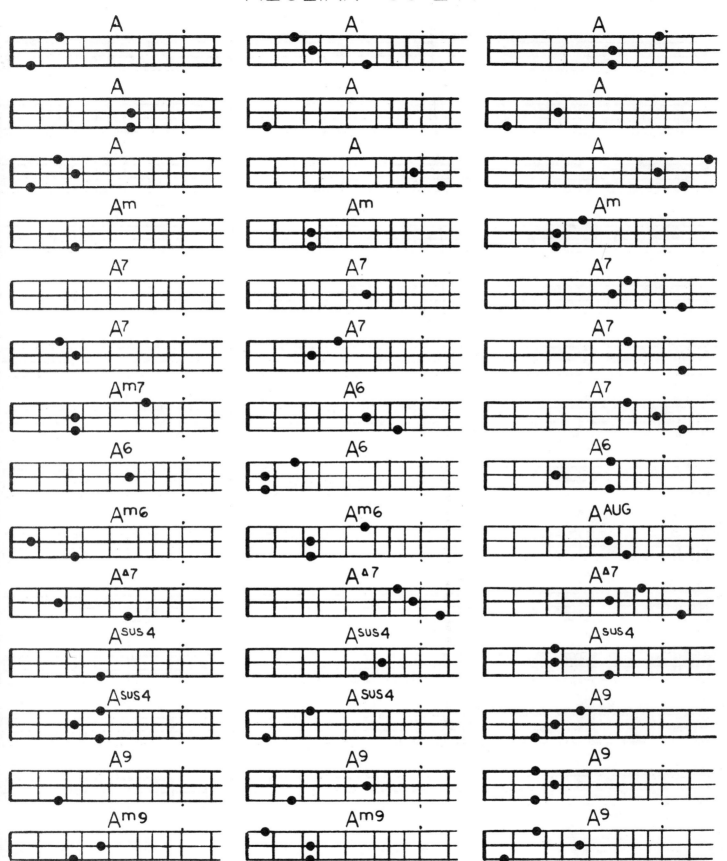

AEOLIAN GG-E-A

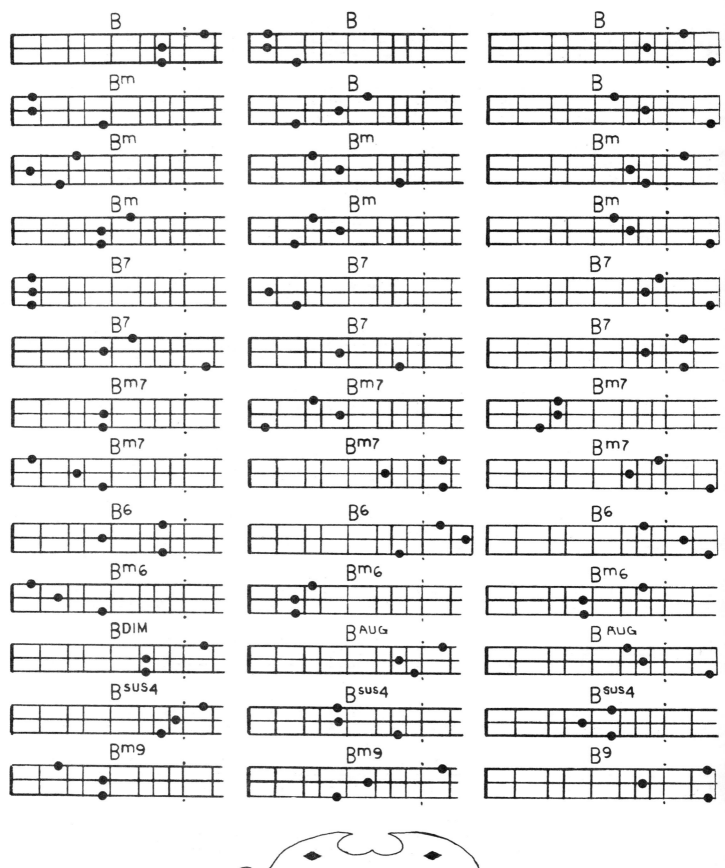

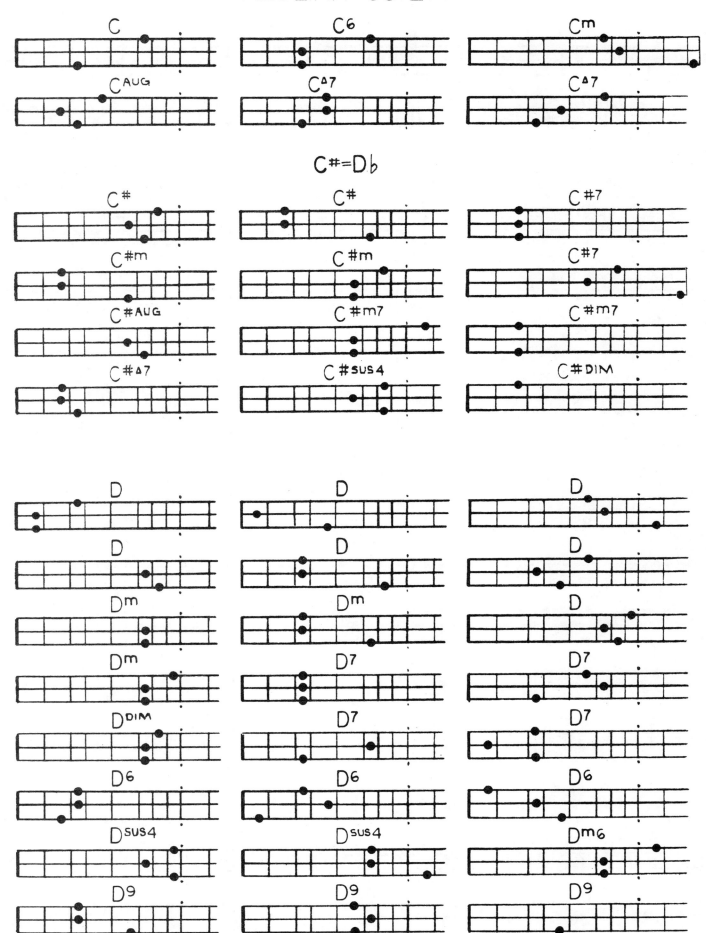

AEOLIAN GG·E·A

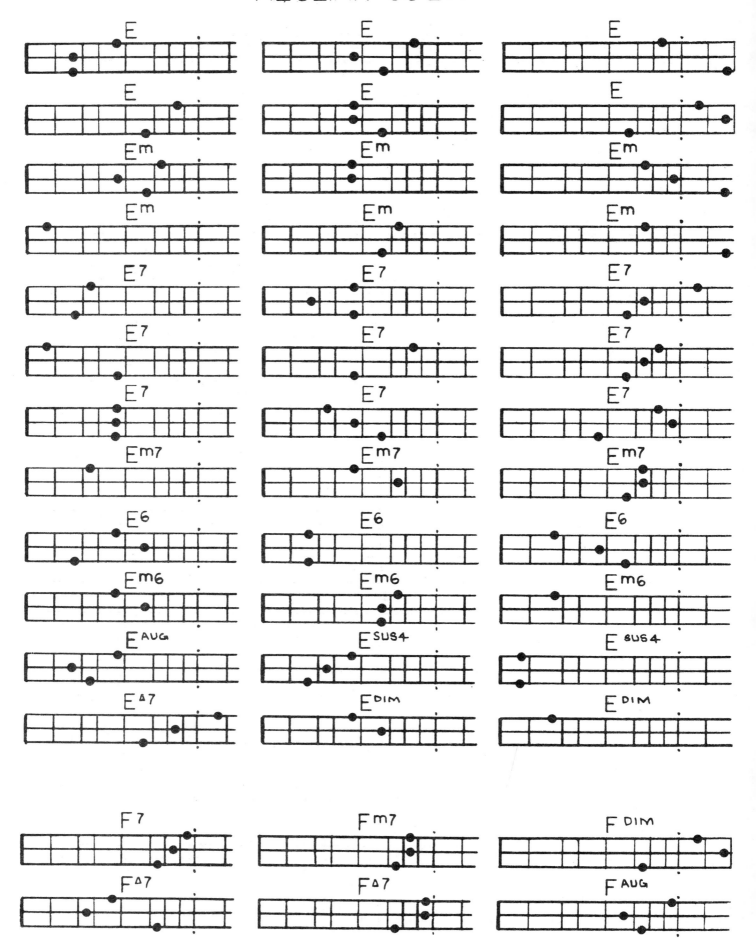

AEOLIAN GGE-A

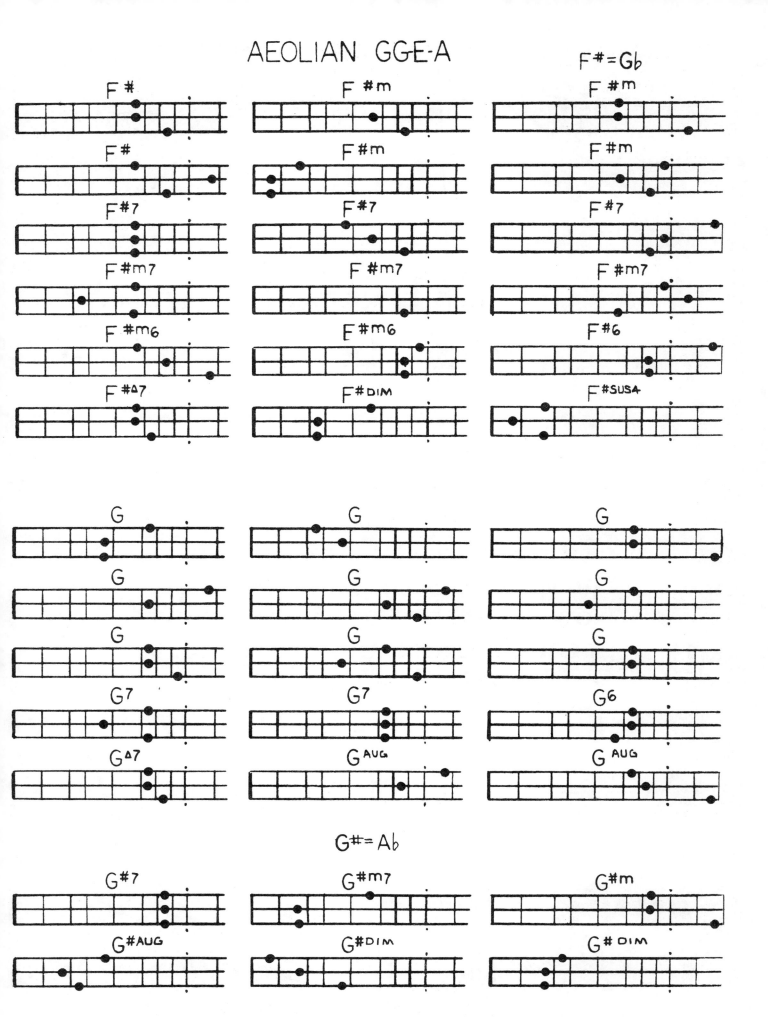

DORIAN
FF - G - C

STRINGS: 1ST   MIDDLE BASS

Tune the Bass String to C below Middle C. Press the Bass String down at the 4th fret and tune the Middle String to this G note. Now press the Bass String down at the 3rd fret and tune the First String(s) to this F note.

DORIAN FF-G-C

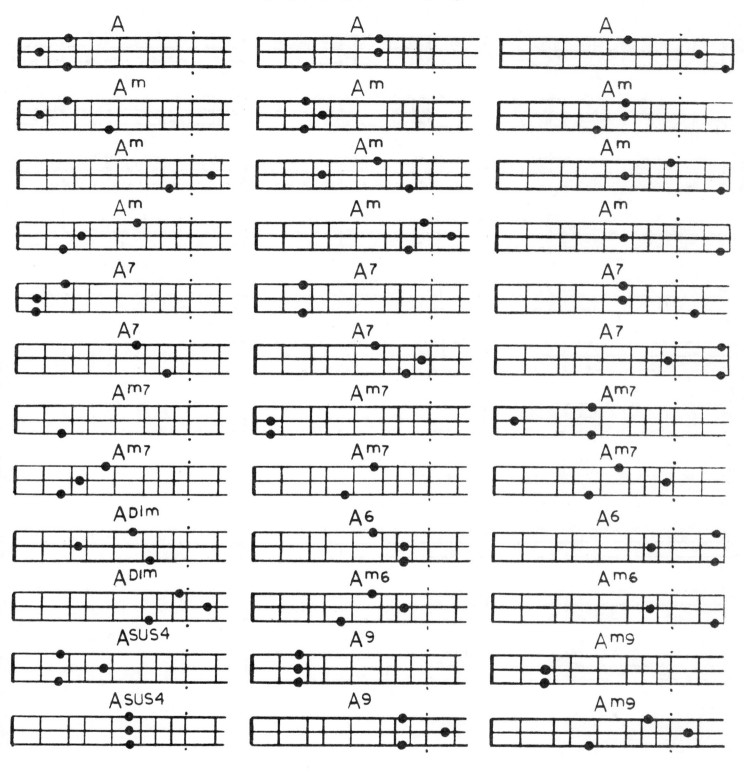

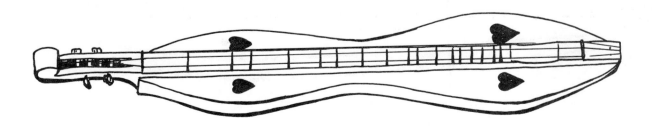

DORIAN FF-G-C

A#=Bb

DORIAN FF-G-C

77

DORIAN F F-G-C

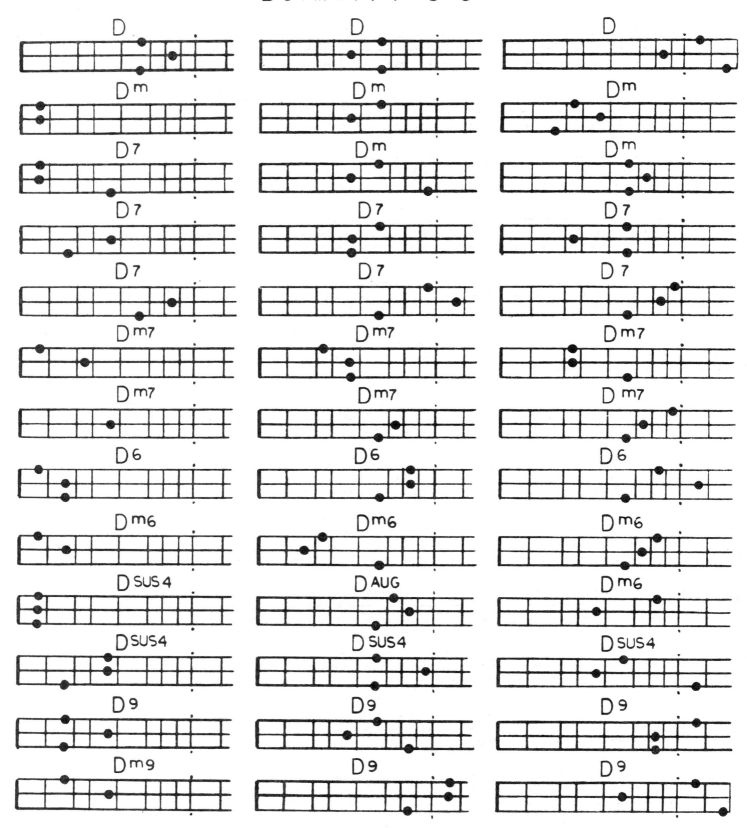

DORIAN FF-G-C

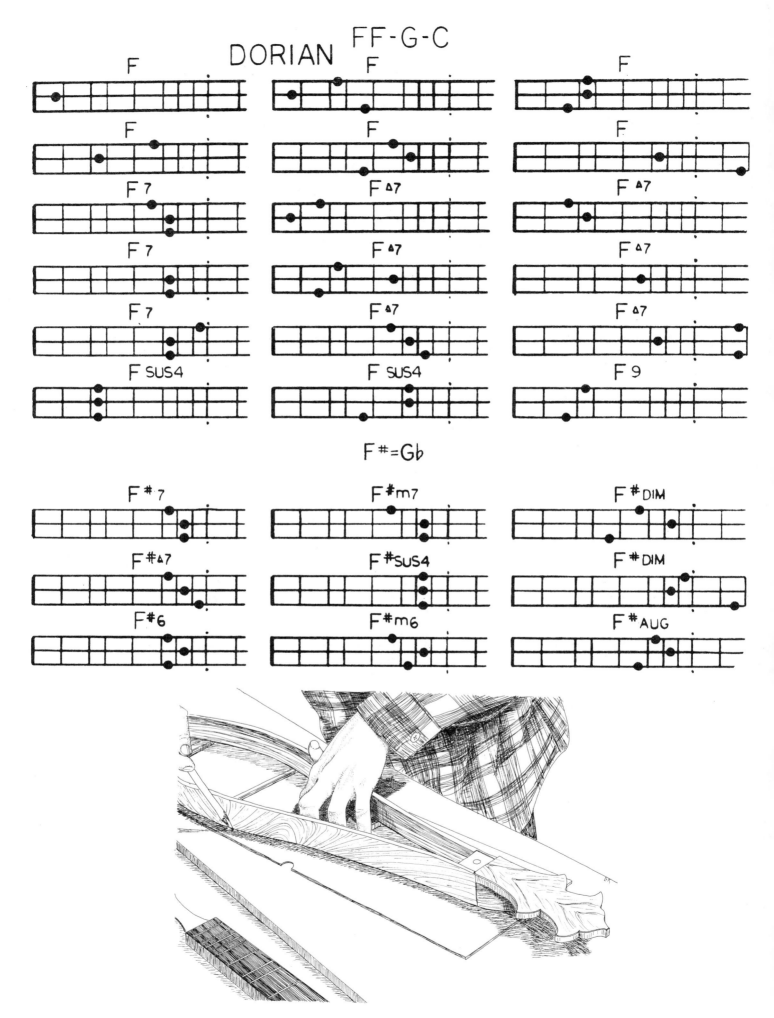

DORIAN FF-G-C

DORIAN
GG - A - D

STRINGS: 1ST   MIDDLE   BASS

Tune the Bass String to D below Middle C. Press the Bass String down at the 4th fret & tune the Middle String to this A note. Now press the Bass String down at the 3rd fret and tune the 1st String(s) to this G note.

DORIAN GG-A-D

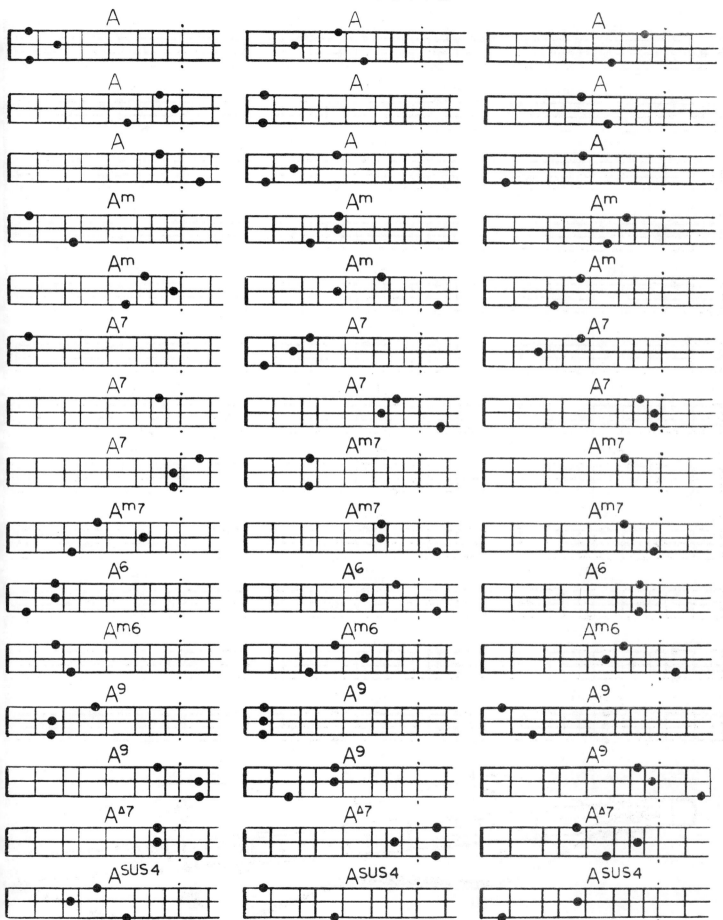

DORIAN GG-A-D

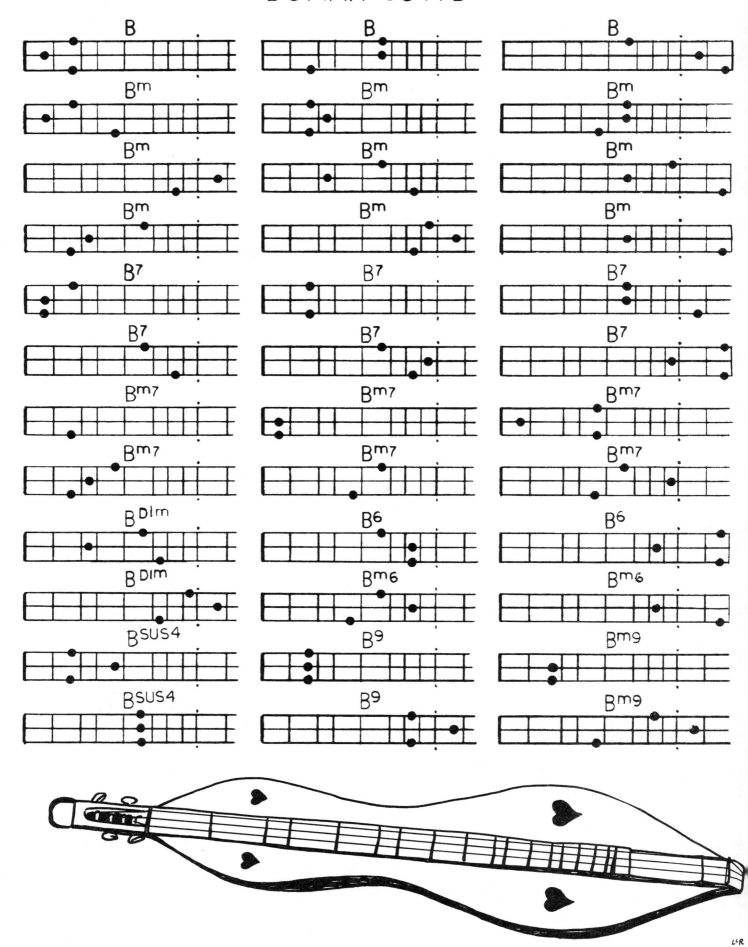

DORIAN GG-A-D

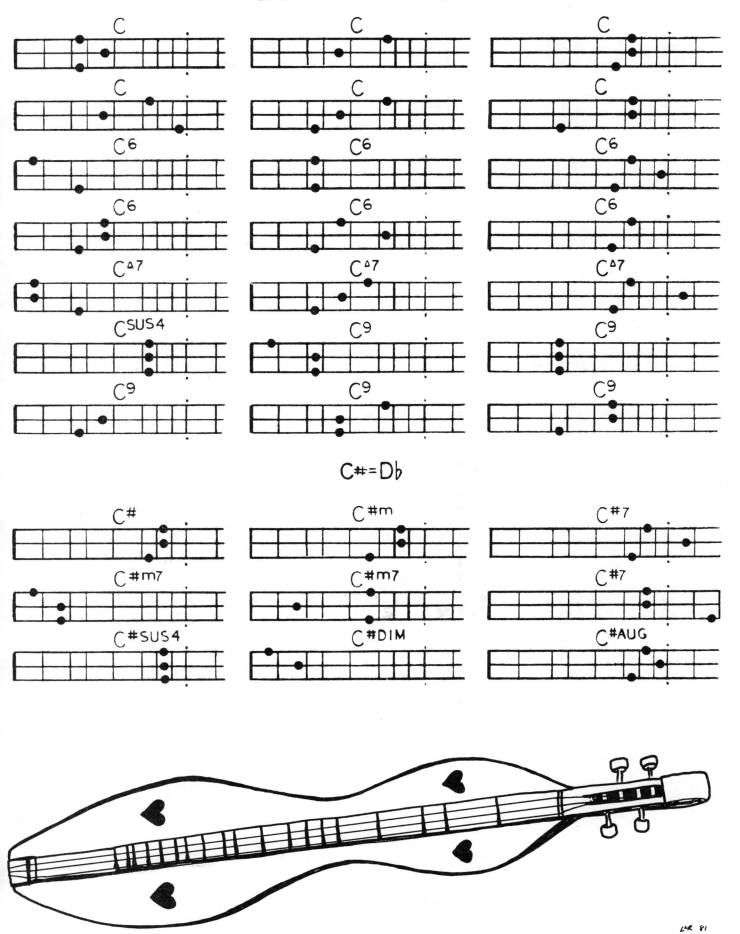

C#=Db

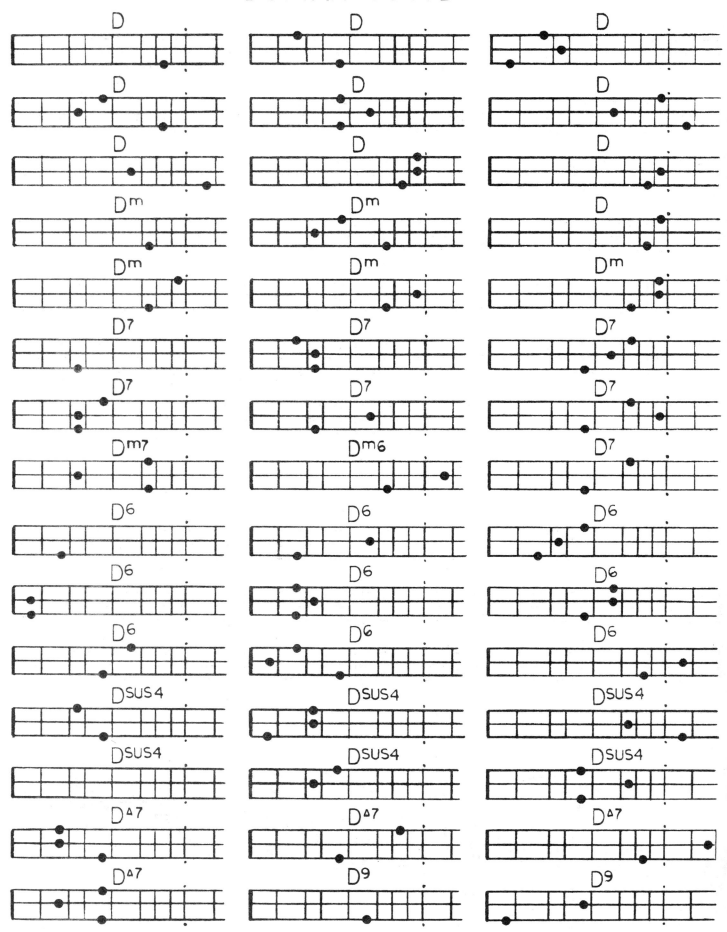

DORIAN GG-A-D

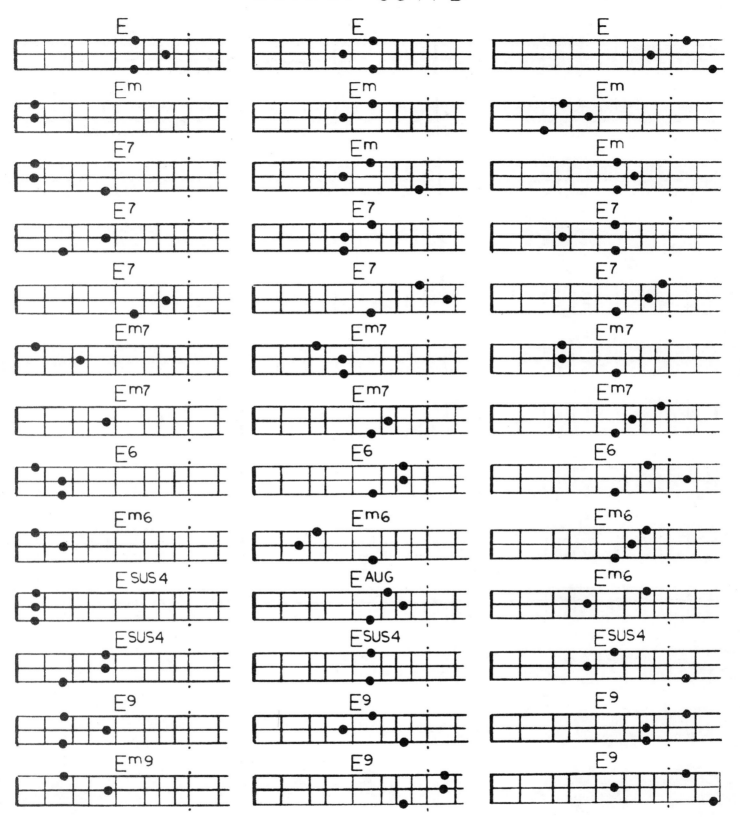

DORIAN GG-A-D

DORIAN GG-A-D

F#=Gb

88

DORIAN GG-A-D

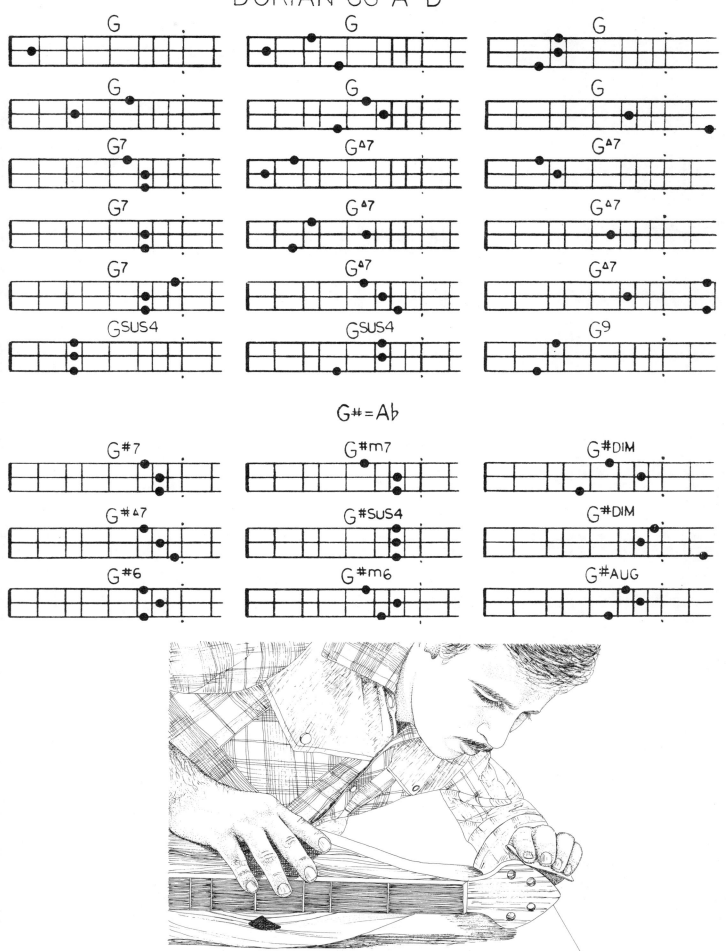

DORIAN
CC - D - G

STRINGS: 1ST   MIDDLE BASS

Tune the Bass String to G below Middle C. Press the Bass String down at the 4th fret & tune the Middle String to this D note. Now press the Bass String down at the 3rd fret and tune the 1st String(s) to this C note.

DORIAN CC-D-G

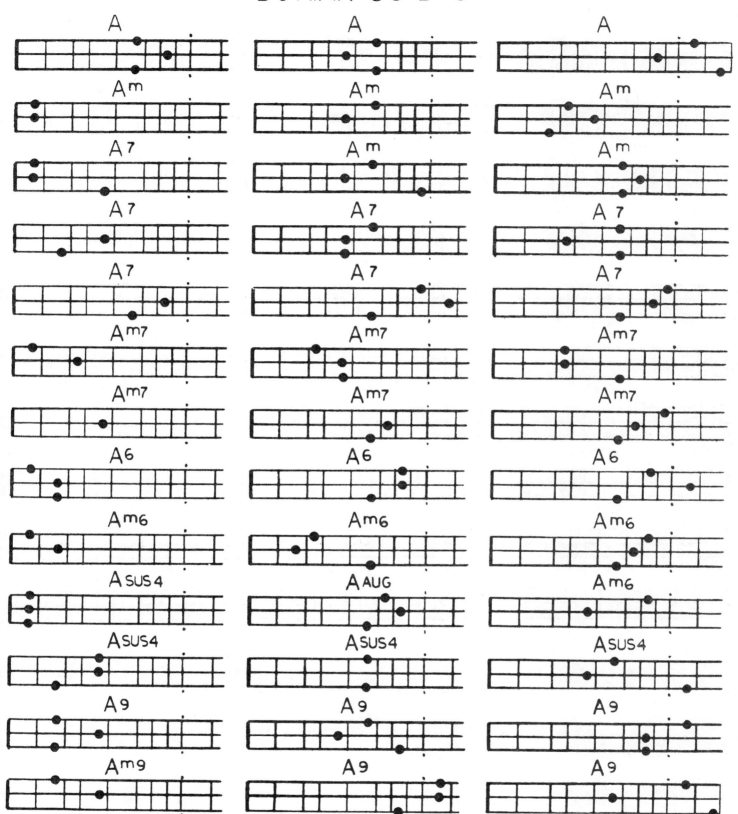

DORIAN CC-D-G   A# = B♭

92

DORIAN CC-D-G

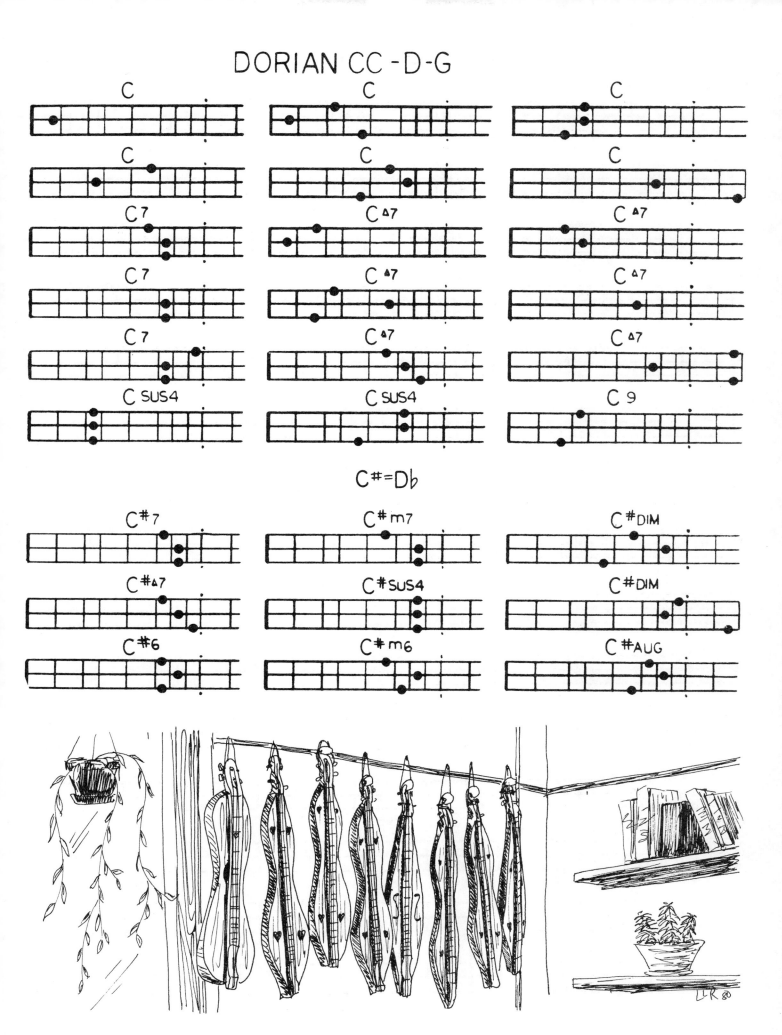

DORIAN CC-D-G

DORIAN CC-D-G

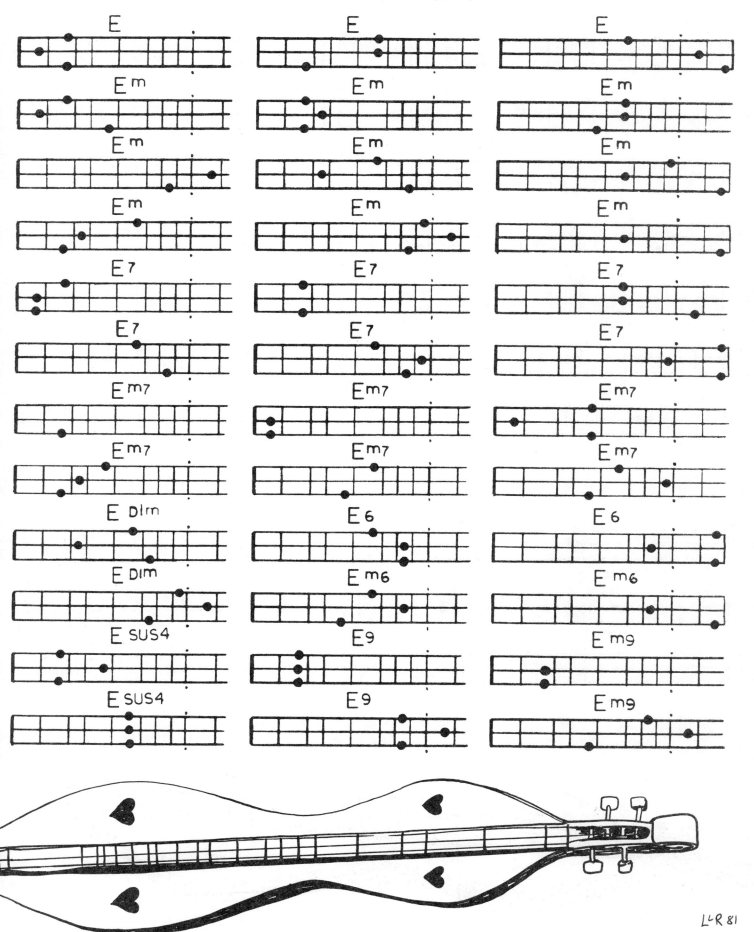

95

DORIAN CC - D - G

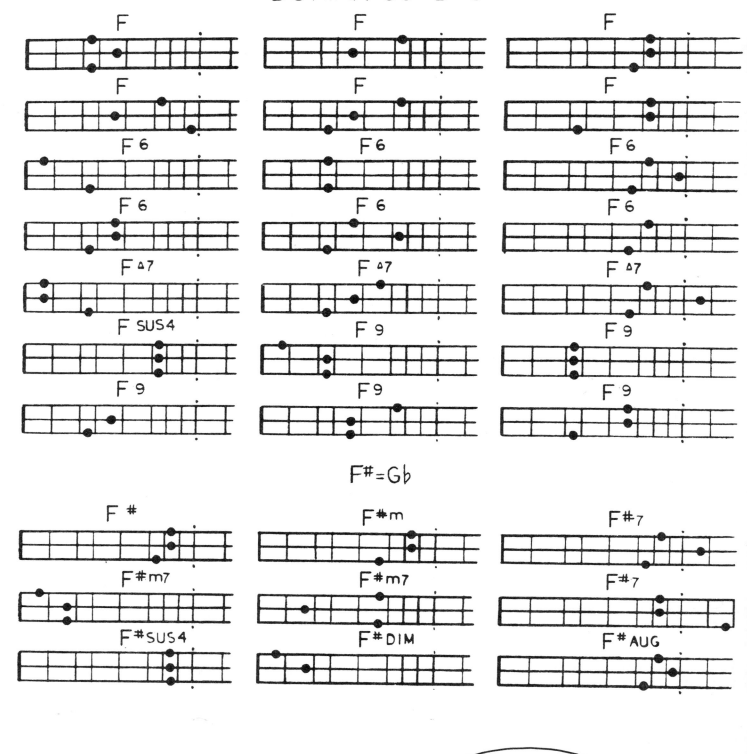

F# = Gb

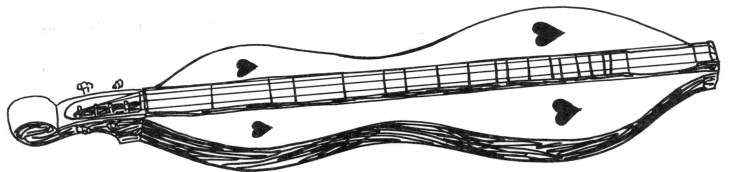

DORIAN CC-D-G

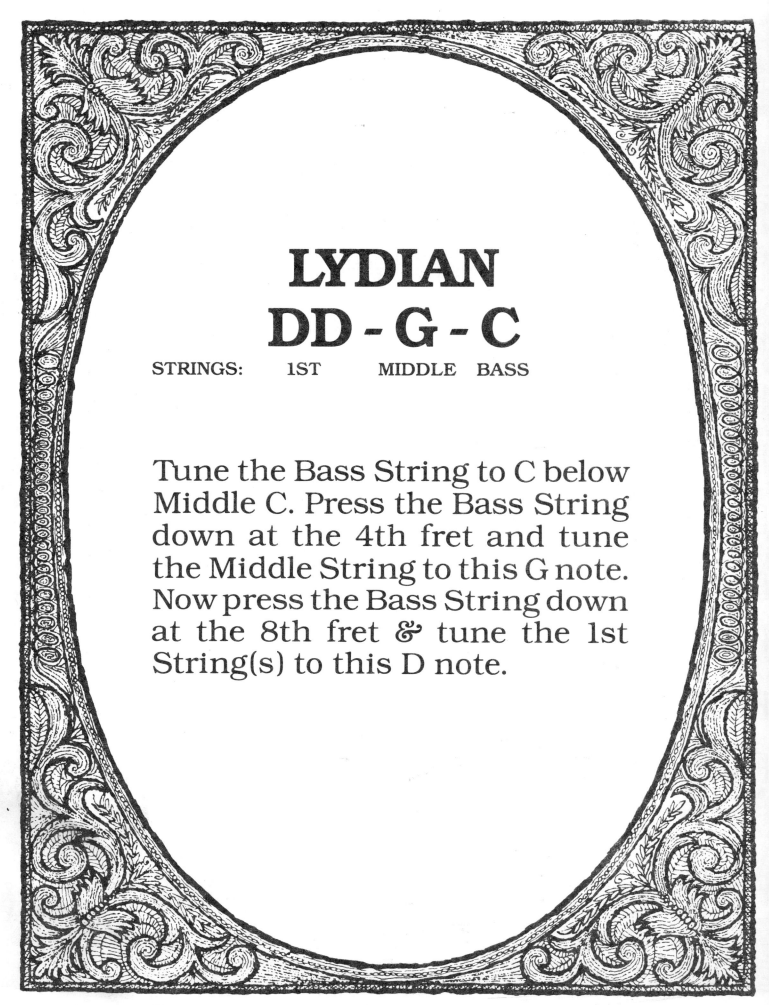

LYDIAN
DD - G - C

STRINGS: 1ST   MIDDLE   BASS

Tune the Bass String to C below Middle C. Press the Bass String down at the 4th fret and tune the Middle String to this G note. Now press the Bass String down at the 8th fret & tune the 1st String(s) to this D note.

LYDIAN DD-G-C

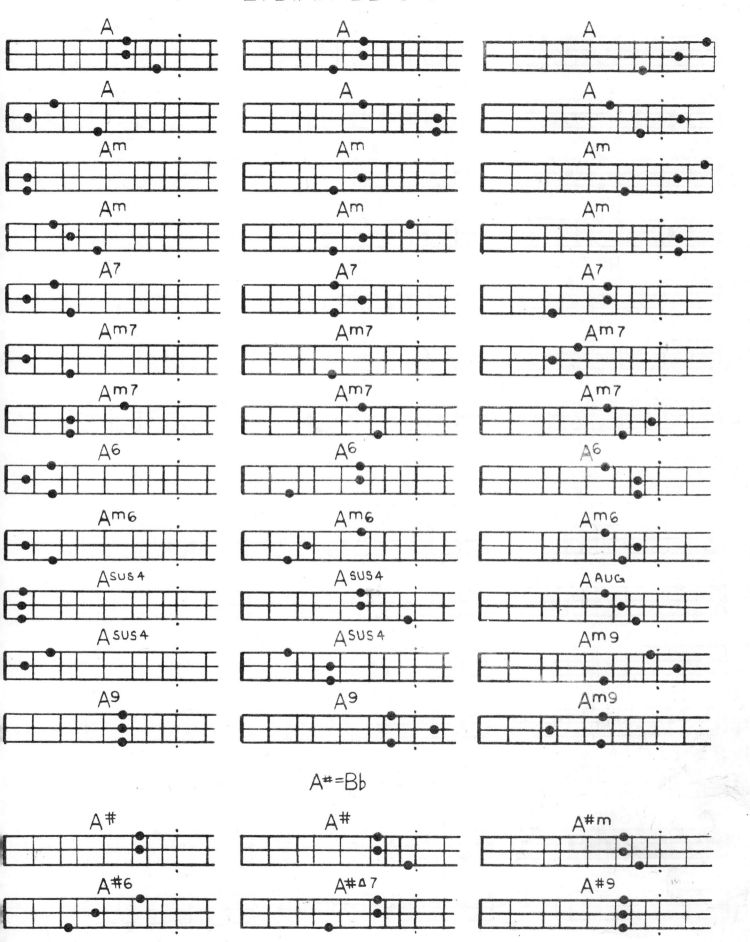

LYDIAN DD-G-C

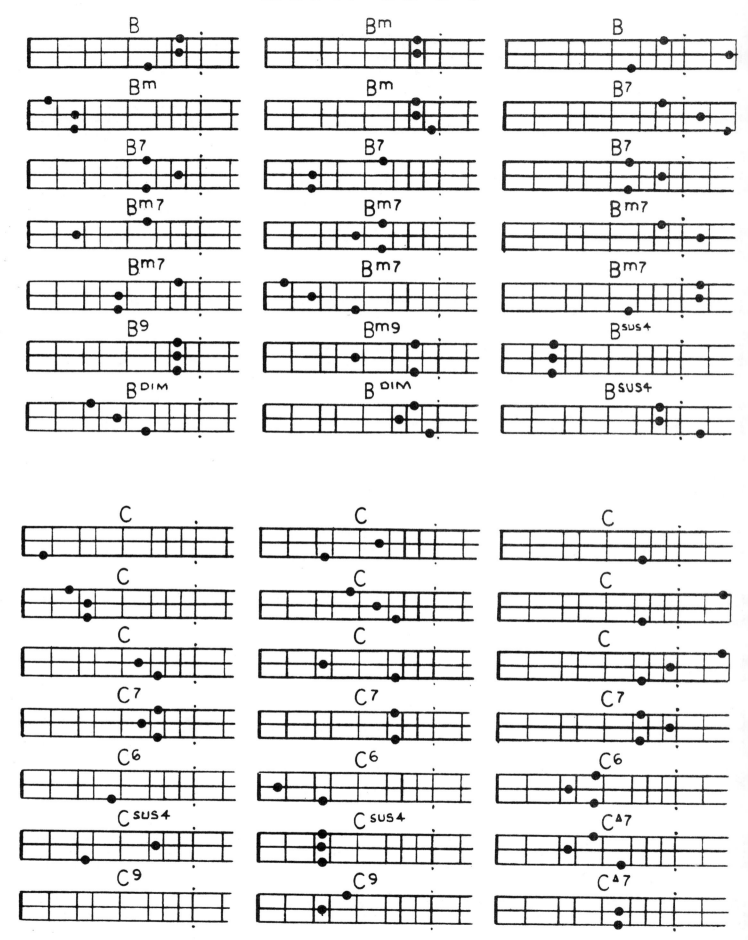

LYDIAN DD-G-C

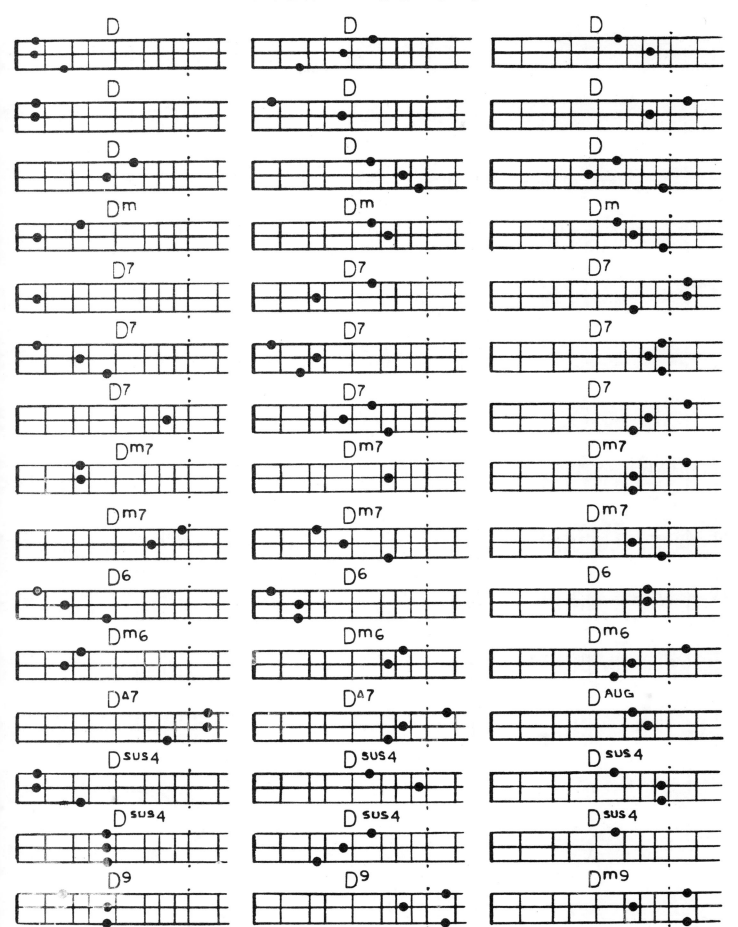

LYDIAN DD-G-C

LYDIAN DD-G-C

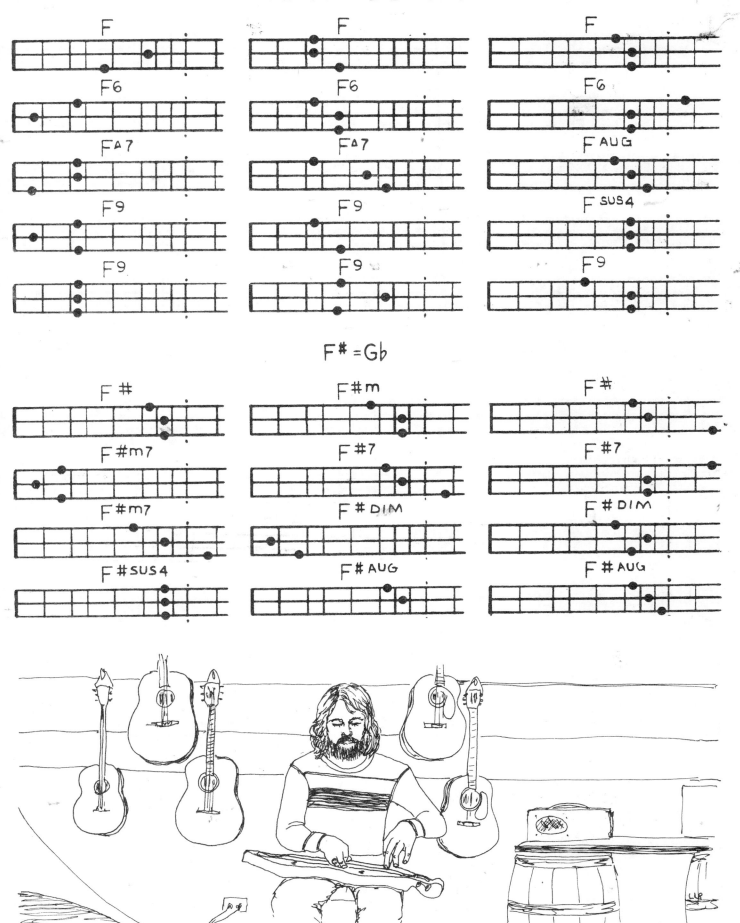

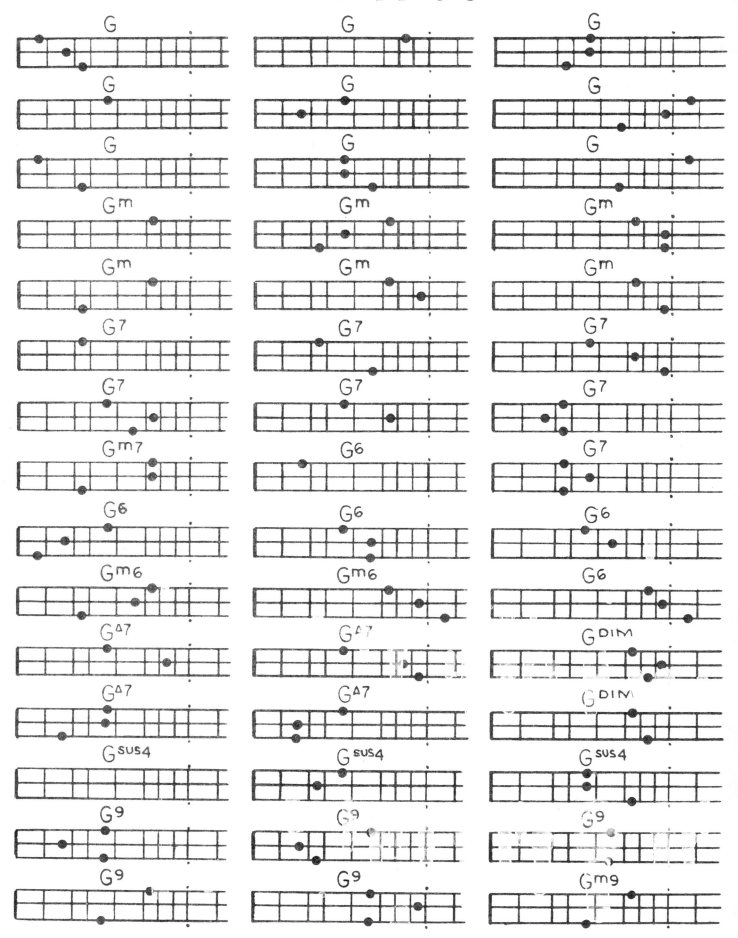

LYDIAN
CC - F - B♭

STRINGS: 1ST   MIDDLE   BASS

Tune the Bass String to B♭ an octave and a whole step below Middle C. Press the Bass String down at the 4th fret and tune the Middle String to this F note. Now press the Bass String down at the 8th fret and tune the 1st String(s) to this C note.

LYDIAN CC - F - B♭

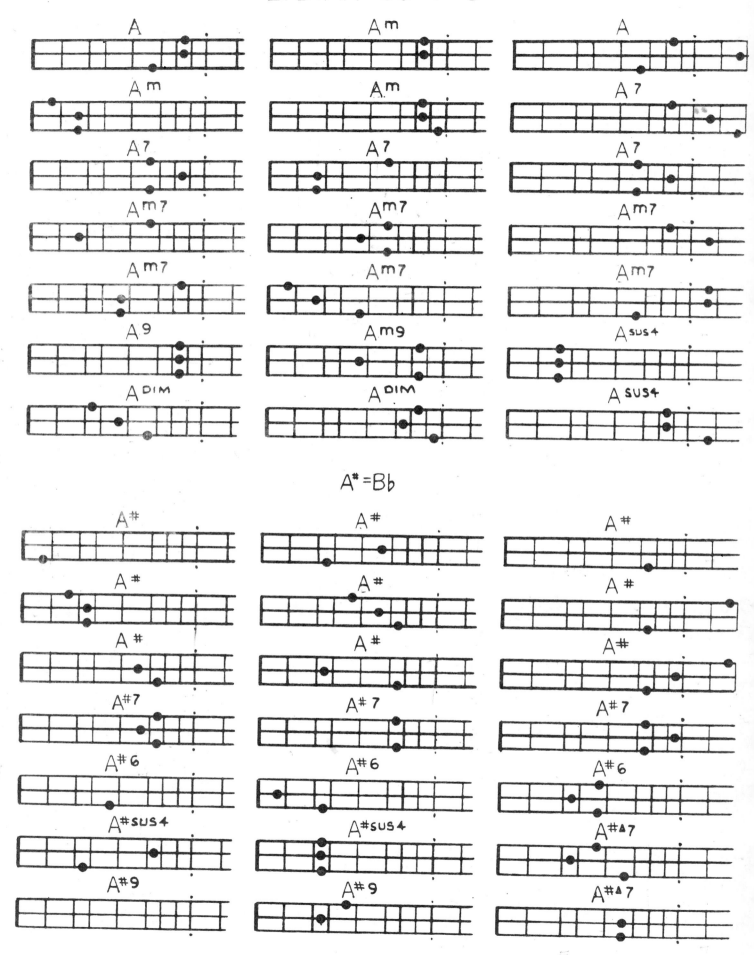

LYDIAN CC-F-B♭

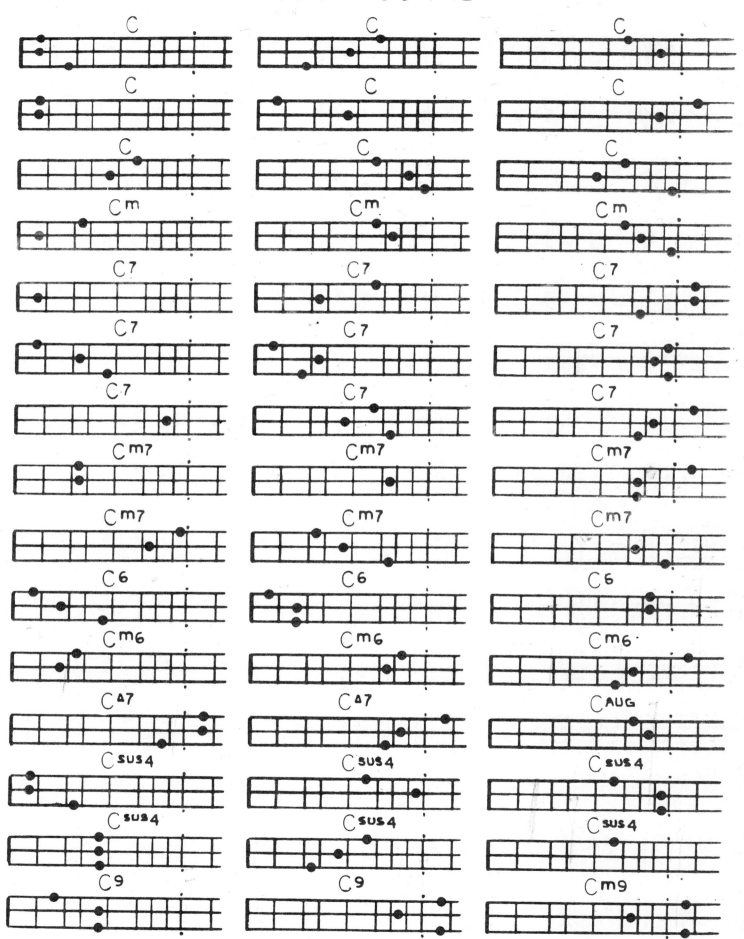

LYDIAN CC-F-B♭

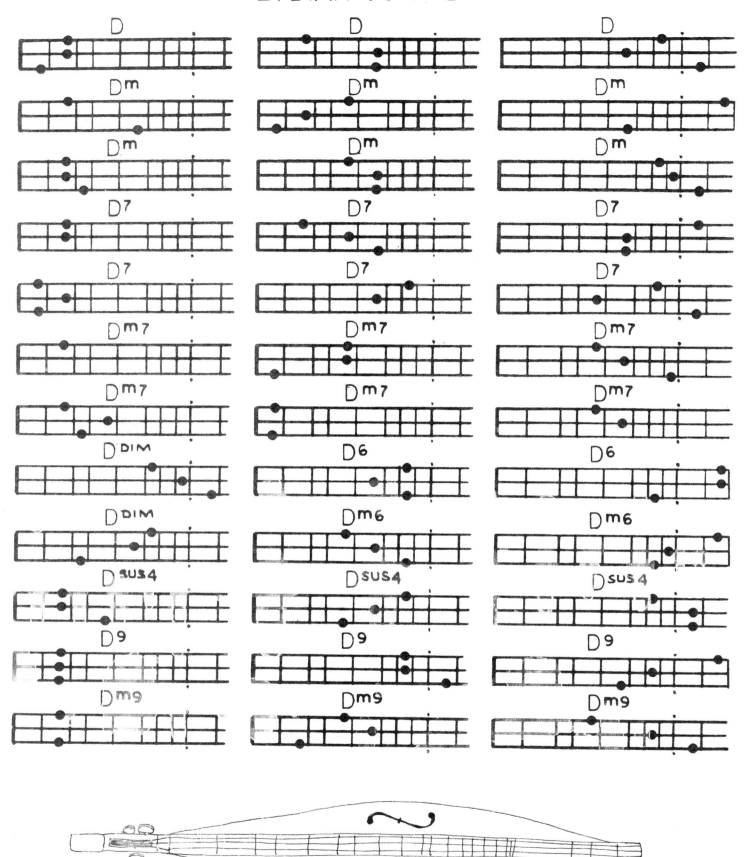

LYDIAN CC-F-B♭

LYDIAN CC -F - B♭

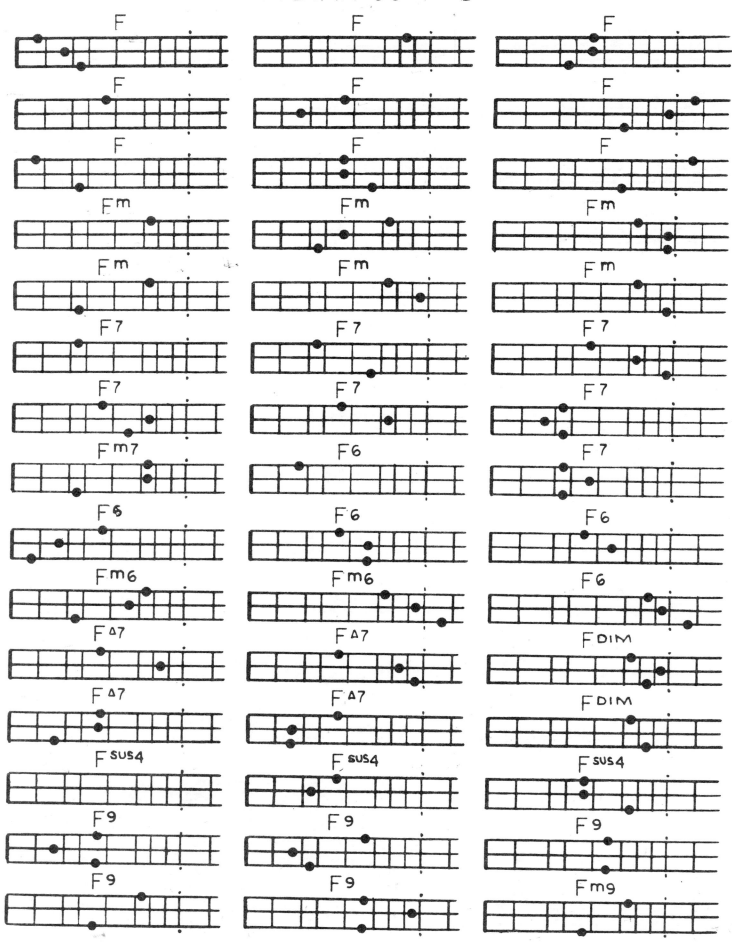

LYDIAN CC-F-B♭

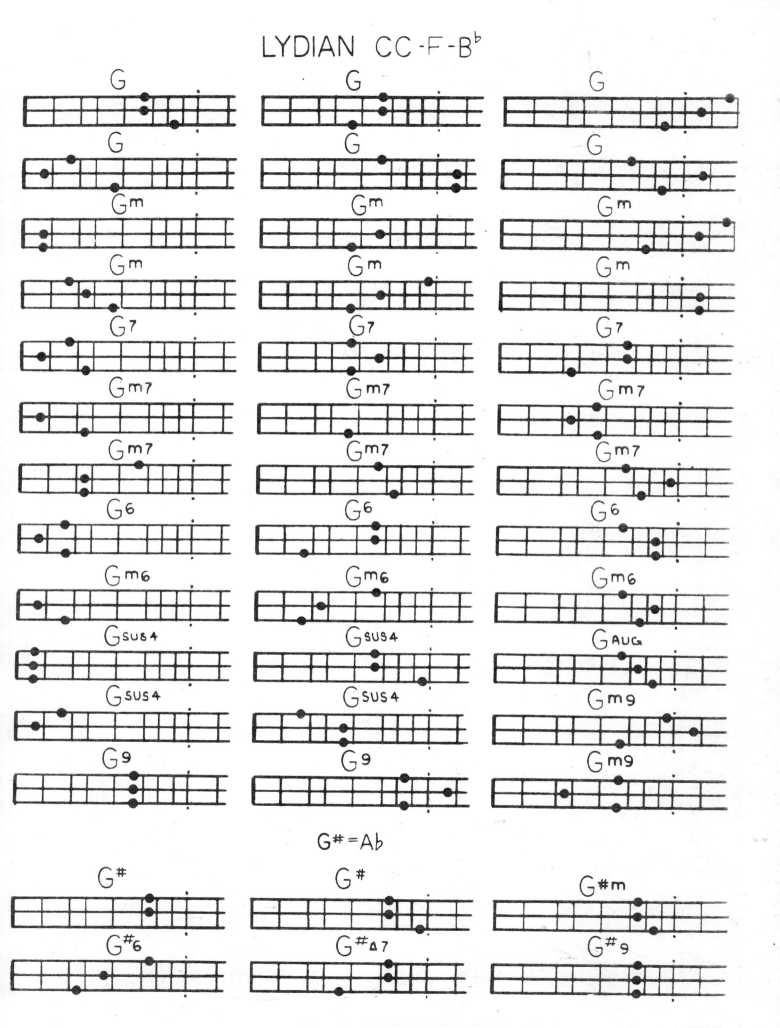

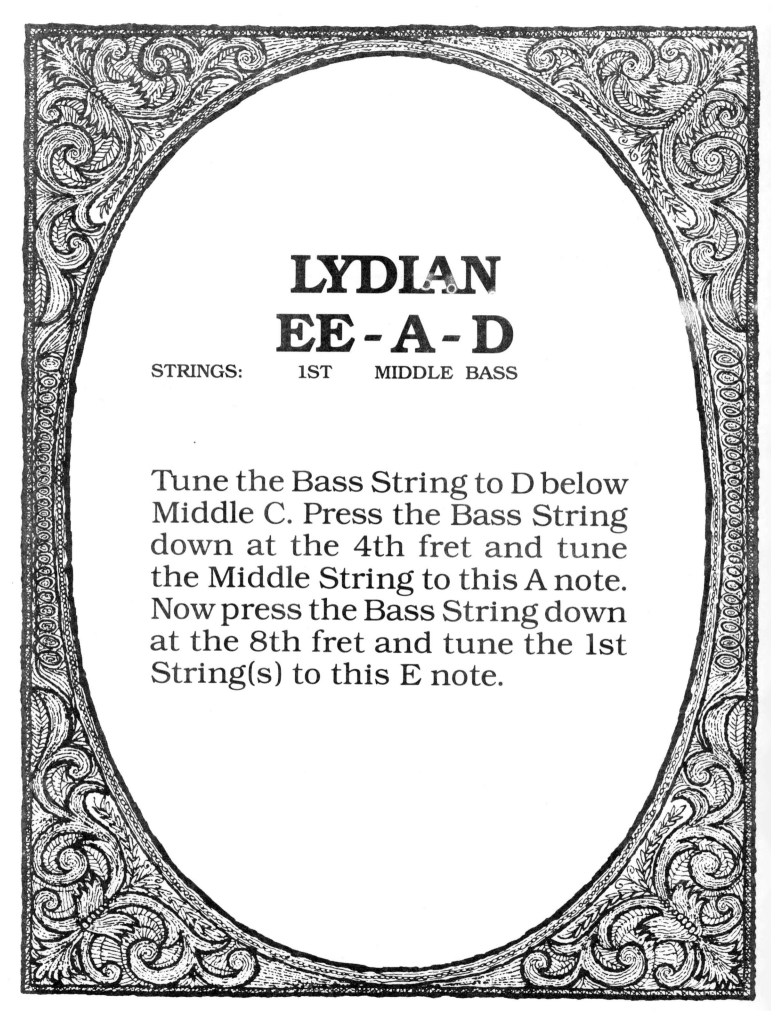

LYDIAN
EE - A - D

STRINGS: 1ST   MIDDLE BASS

Tune the Bass String to D below Middle C. Press the Bass String down at the 4th fret and tune the Middle String to this A note. Now press the Bass String down at the 8th fret and tune the 1st String(s) to this E note.

LYDIAN EE-A-D

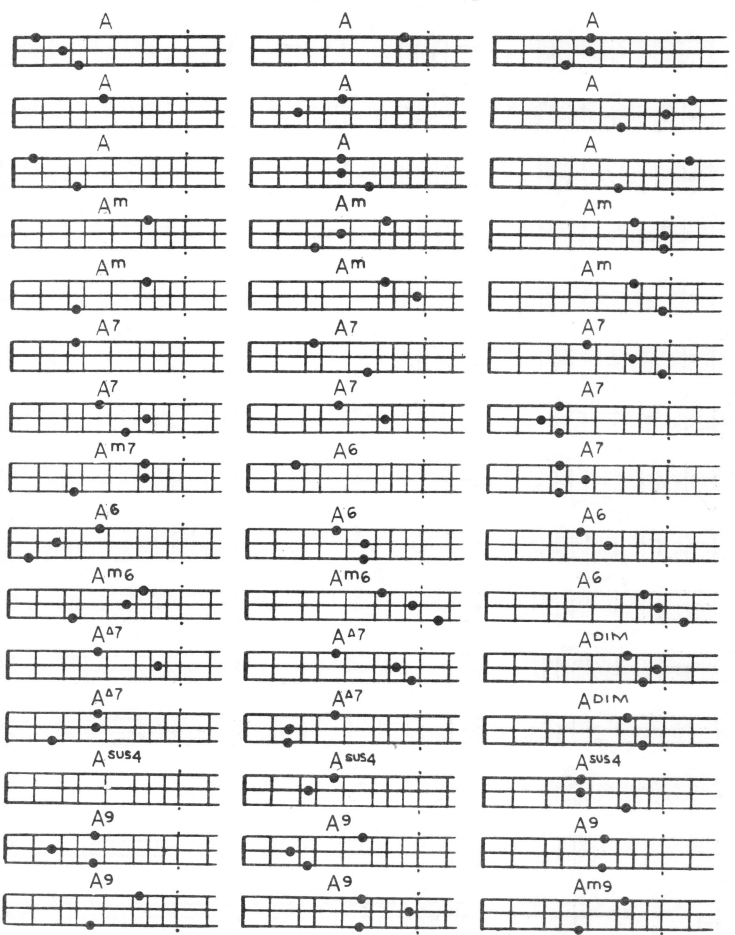

LYDIAN EE-A-D

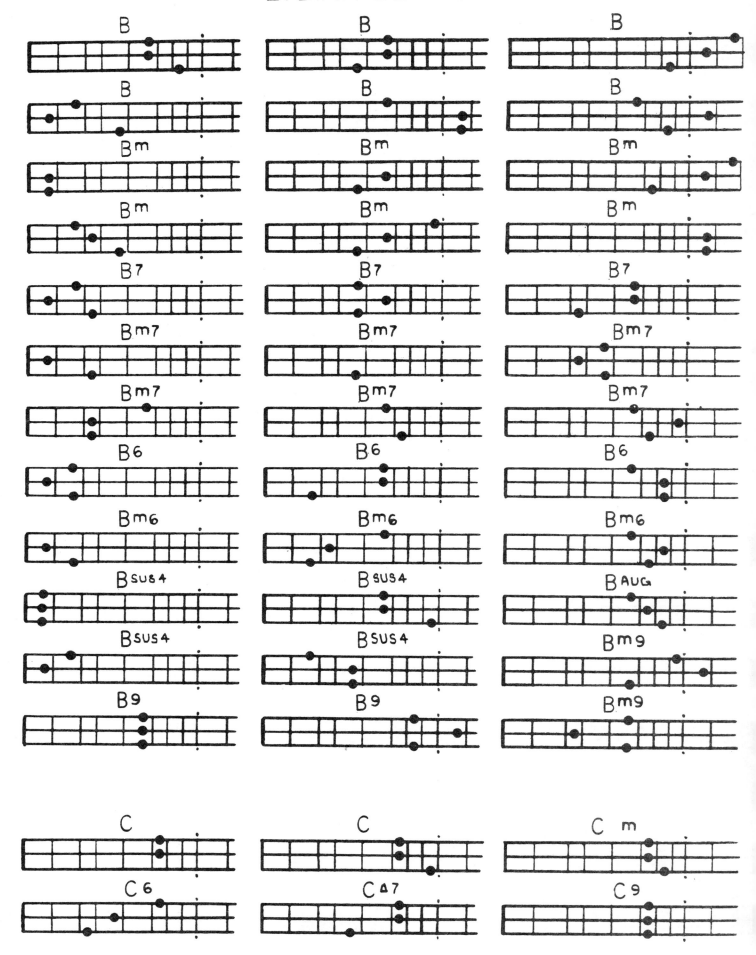

LYDIAN EE-A-D

C#=Db

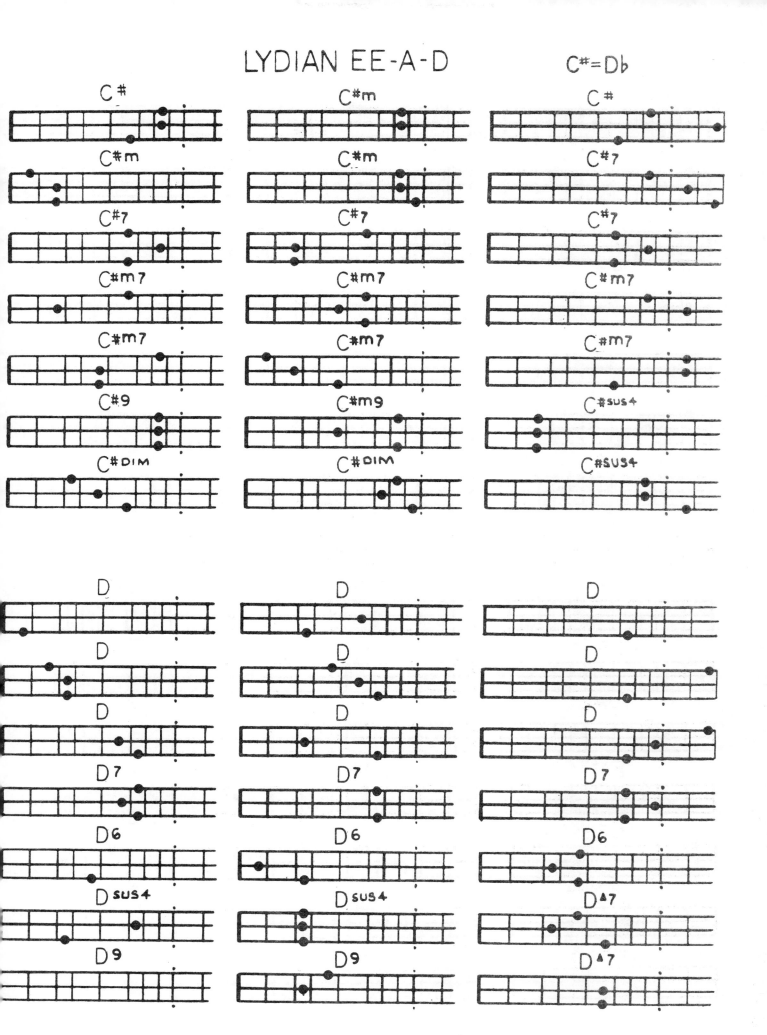

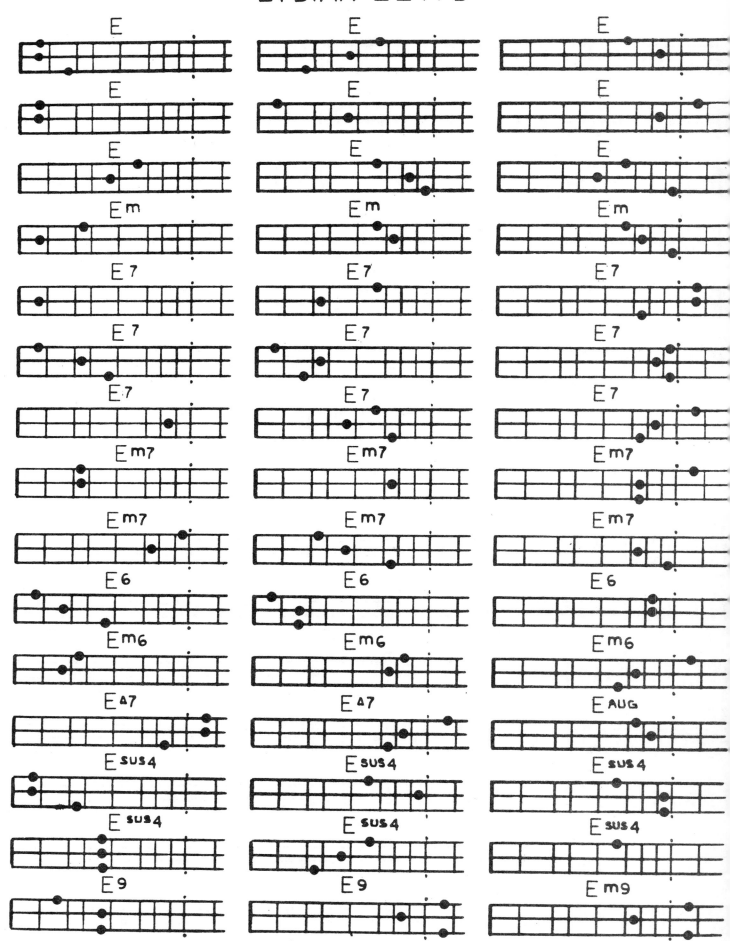

LYDIAN EE-A-D

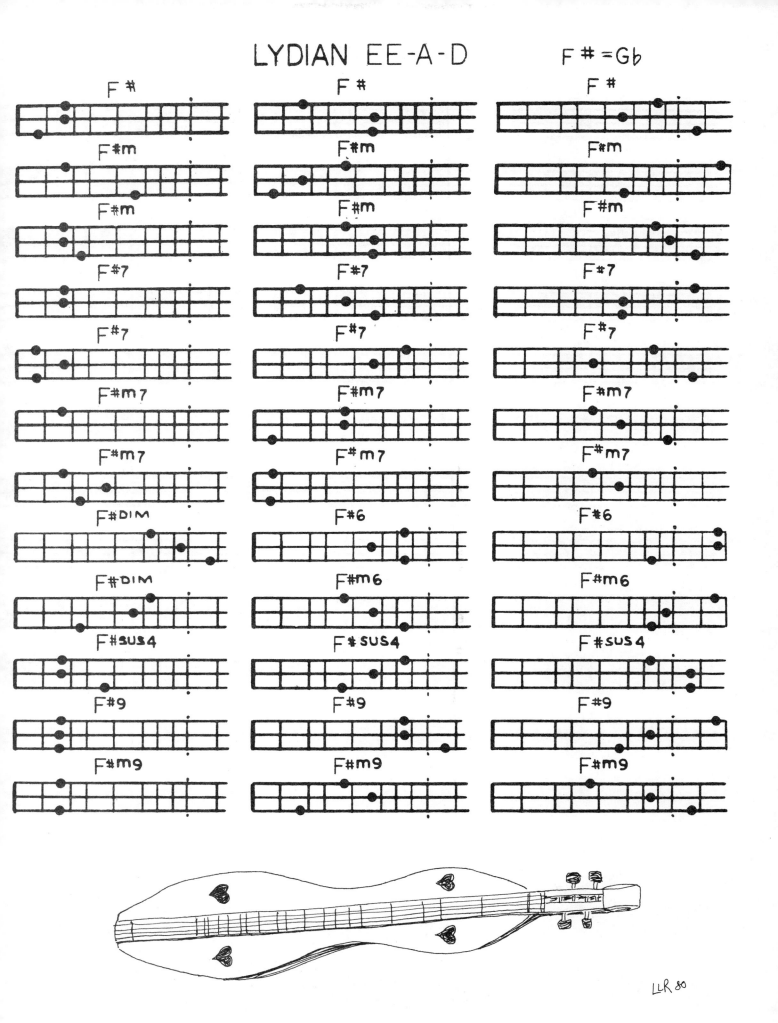

LYDIAN EE-A-D

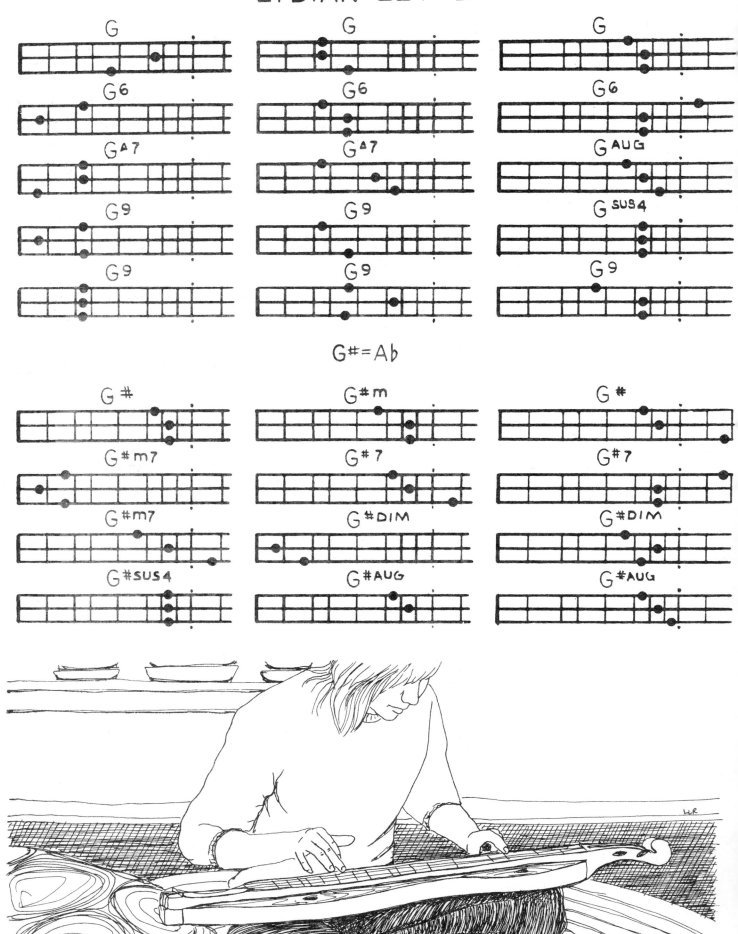

PHRYGIAN
B♭ B♭ - D - G

STRING: 1ST   MIDDLE BASS

Tune the Bass String to G below Middle C. Press the Bass String down at the 4th fret and tune the Middle String to this D note. Now press the 1st String(s) down at the 2nd fret and tune the 1st String(s) to the D note heard on the Middle String. While tuning to the Middle String keep the 1st String(s) depressed on the 2nd fret.

PHRYGIAN B♭B♭-D-G

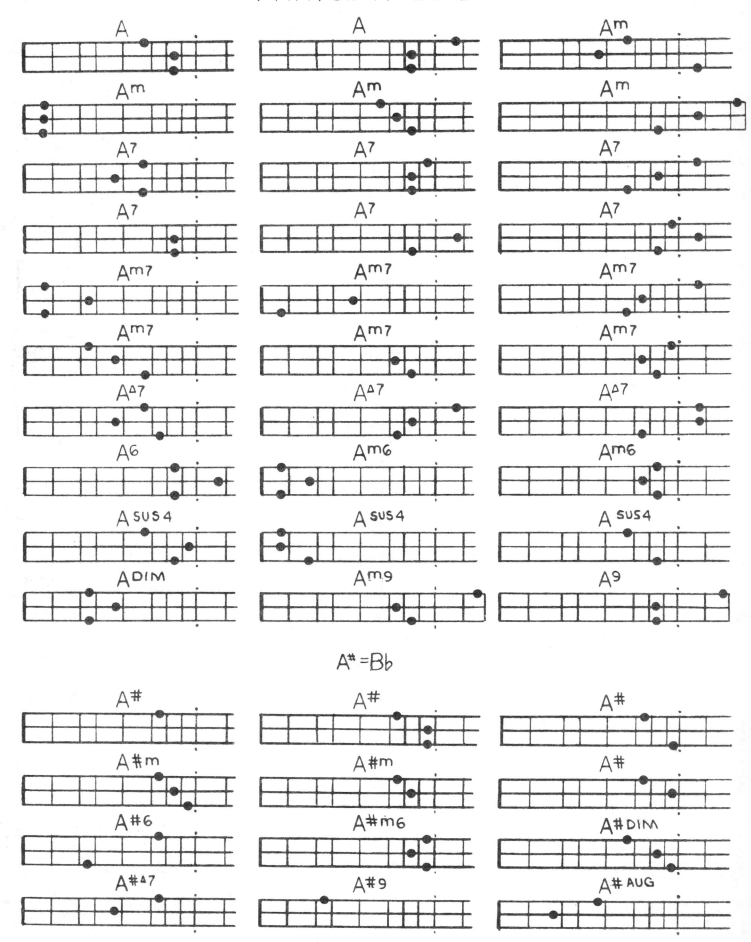

A♯ = B♭

PHRYGIAN B♭B♭-D-G

121

PHRYGIAN B♭B♭D-G

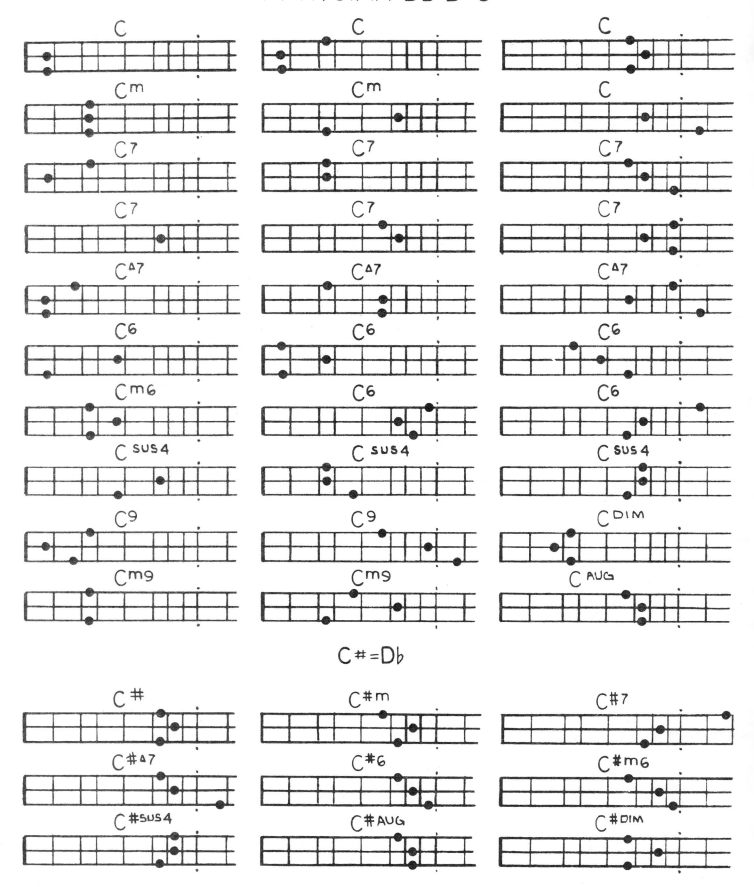

122

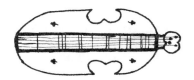

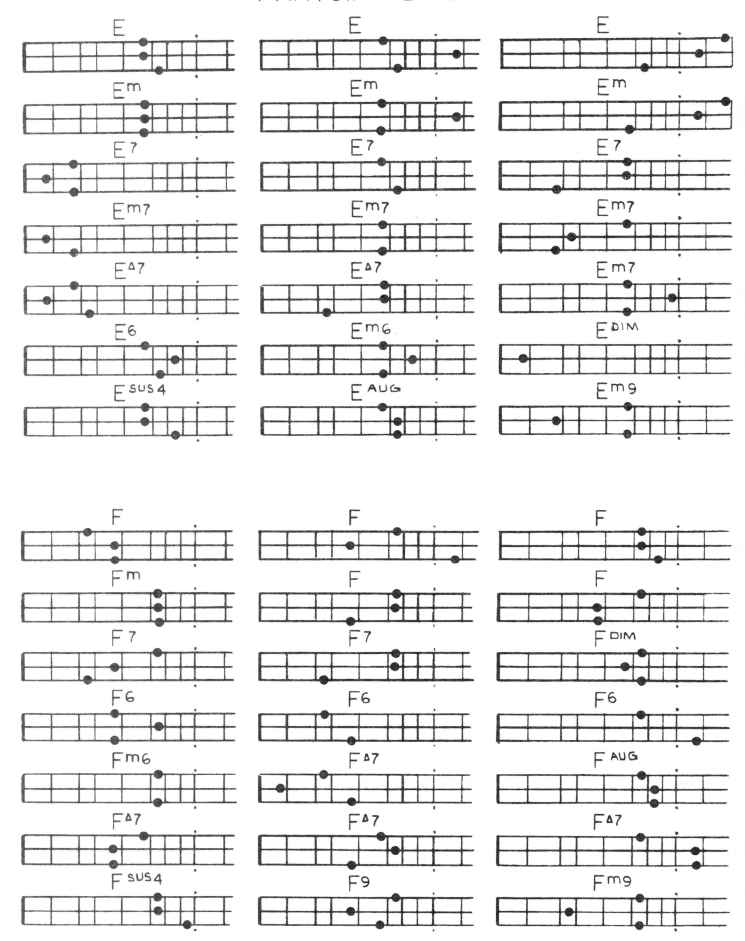

PHRYGIAN B♭·B♭·D·G   F#=G♭

PHRYGIAN
FF - A - D

STRINGS: 1ST   MIDDLE   BASS

Tune the Bass String to D below Middle C. Press the Bass String down at the 4th fret and tune the Middle String to this A note. Now press the 1st String(s) down at the 2nd fret and tune the 1st String(s) to the A note heard on the Middle String, or 1 octave above. While tuning to the Middle String, keep the 1st String depressed at the 2nd fret.

PHRYGIAN FF-A-D

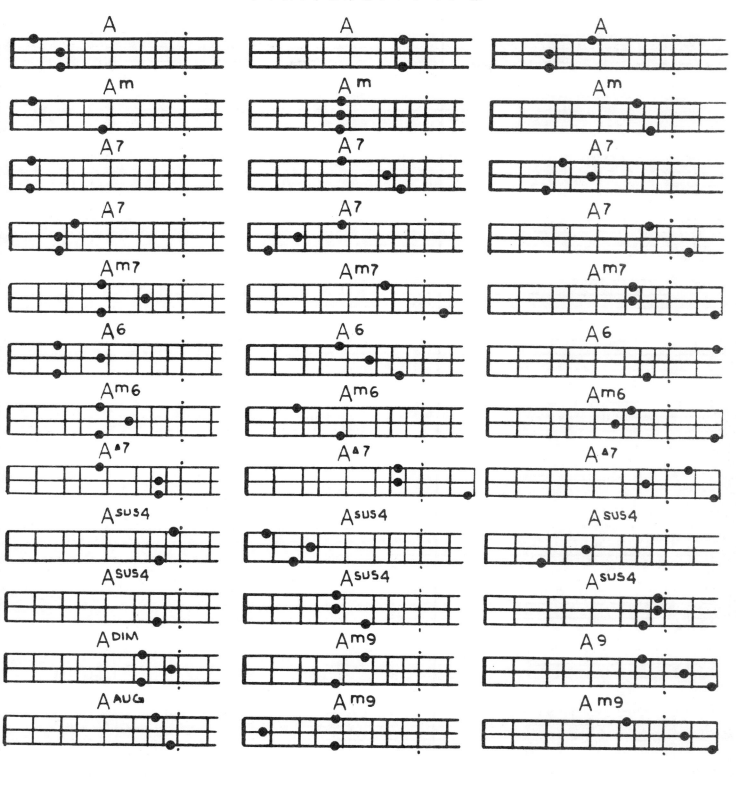

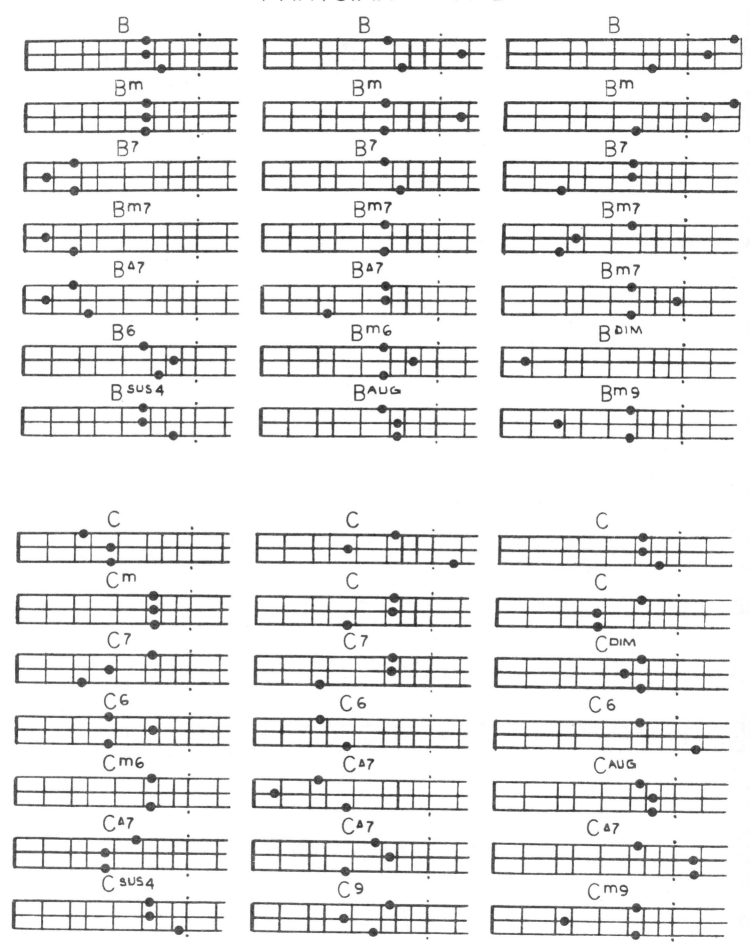

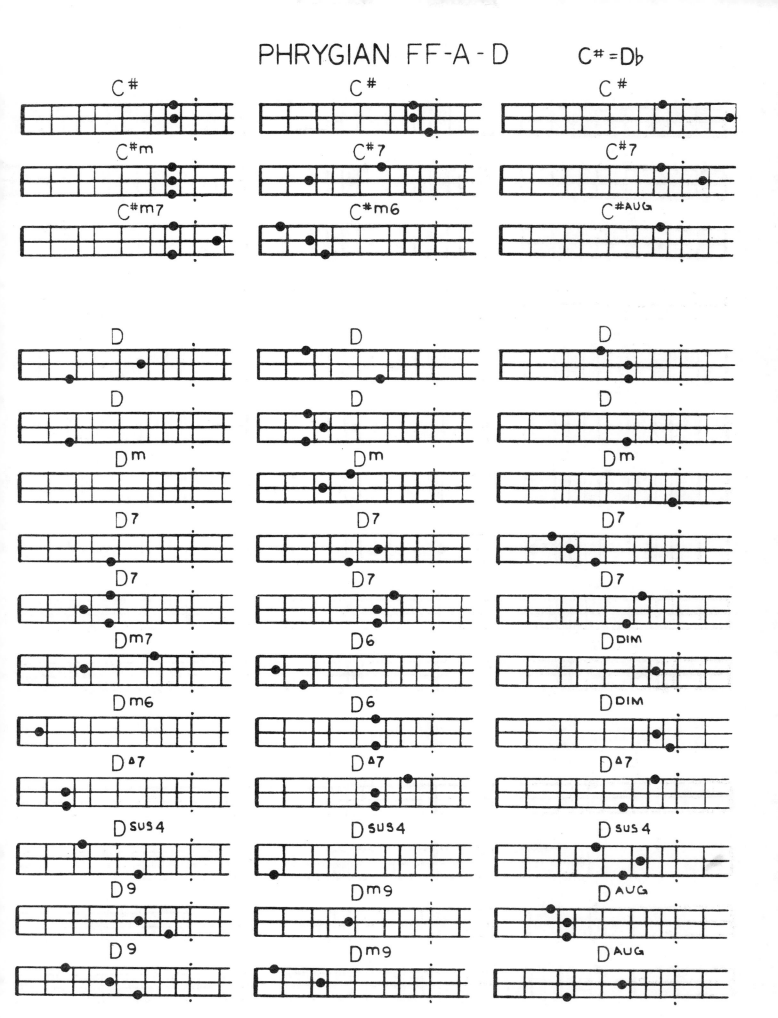

PHRYGIAN FF-A-D

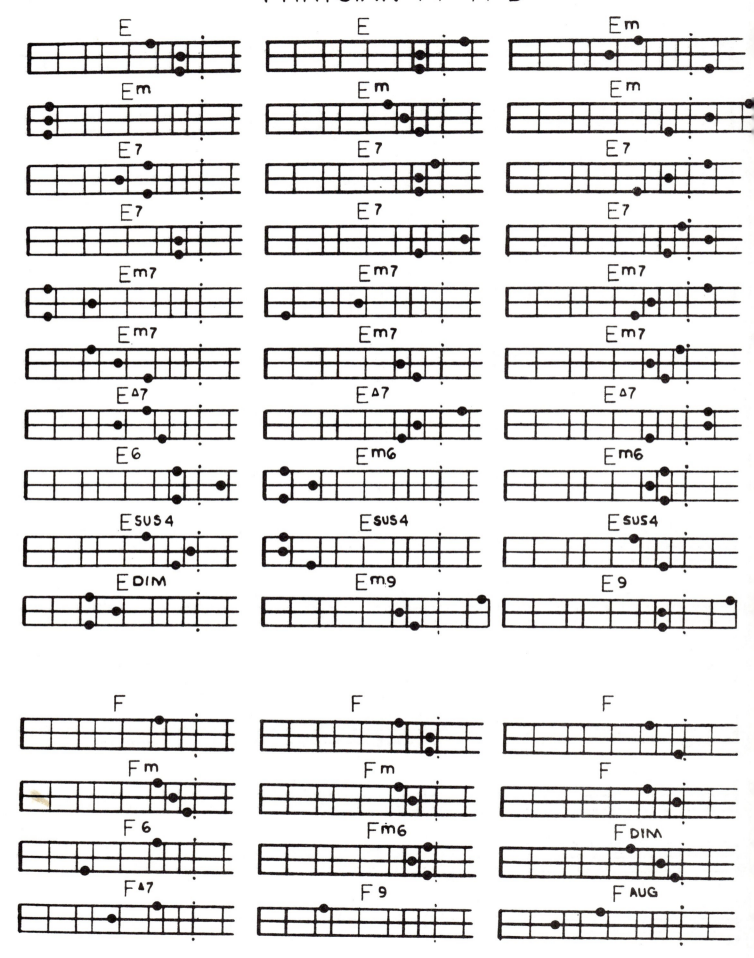

PHRYGIAN FF-A-D   F#=Gb

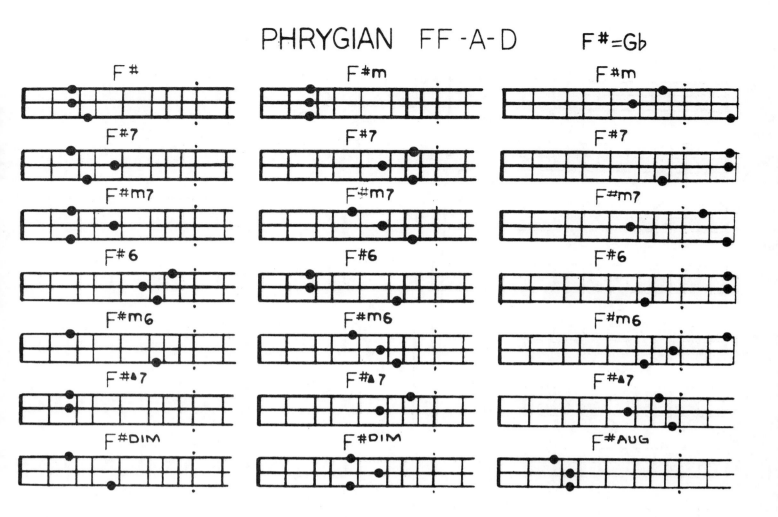

131

PHRYGIAN FF-A-D

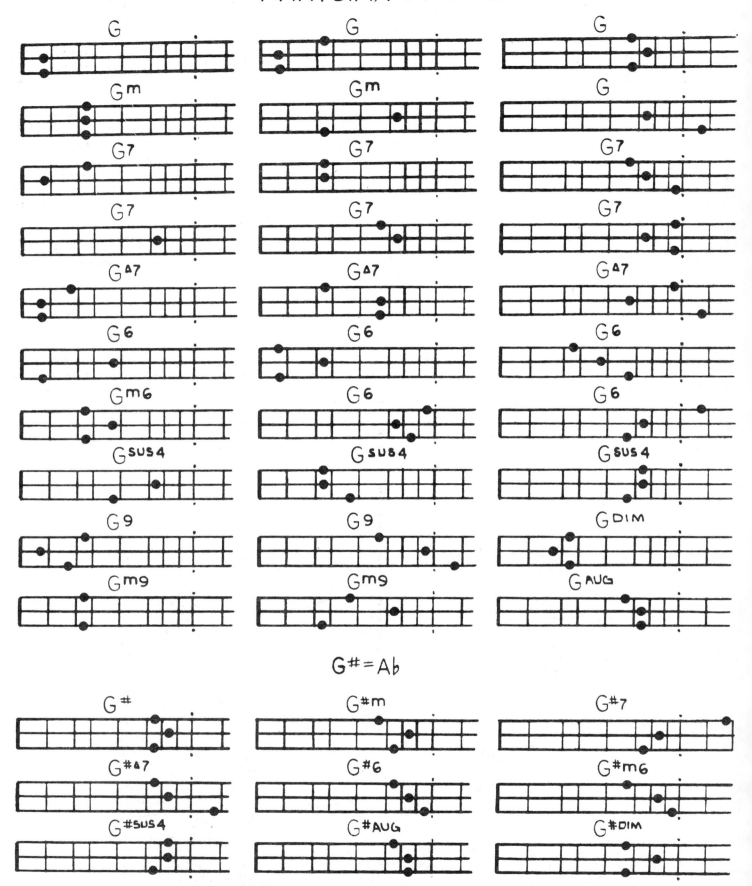

PHRYGIAN
E♭ E♭ - G - C

STRINGS: 1ST   MIDDLE BASS

Tune the Bass String to C below Middle C. Press the Bass String down at the 4th fret and tune the Middle String to this G note. Now press the 1st String(s) down at the 2nd fret and tune the First String(s) up an octave above the G note heard on the Middle String. While tuning to the Middle String, keep the 1st String(s) depressed at the 2nd fret.

PHRYGIAN E♭ E♭ G-C

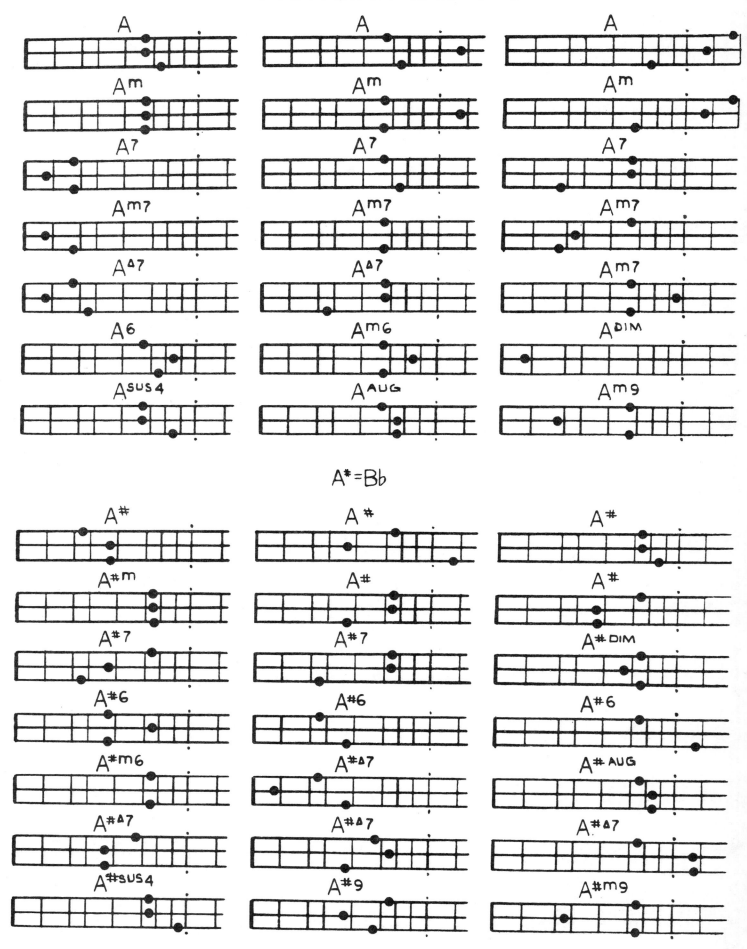

PHRYGIAN E♭E♭-G-C

PHRYGIAN E♭E♭-G-C

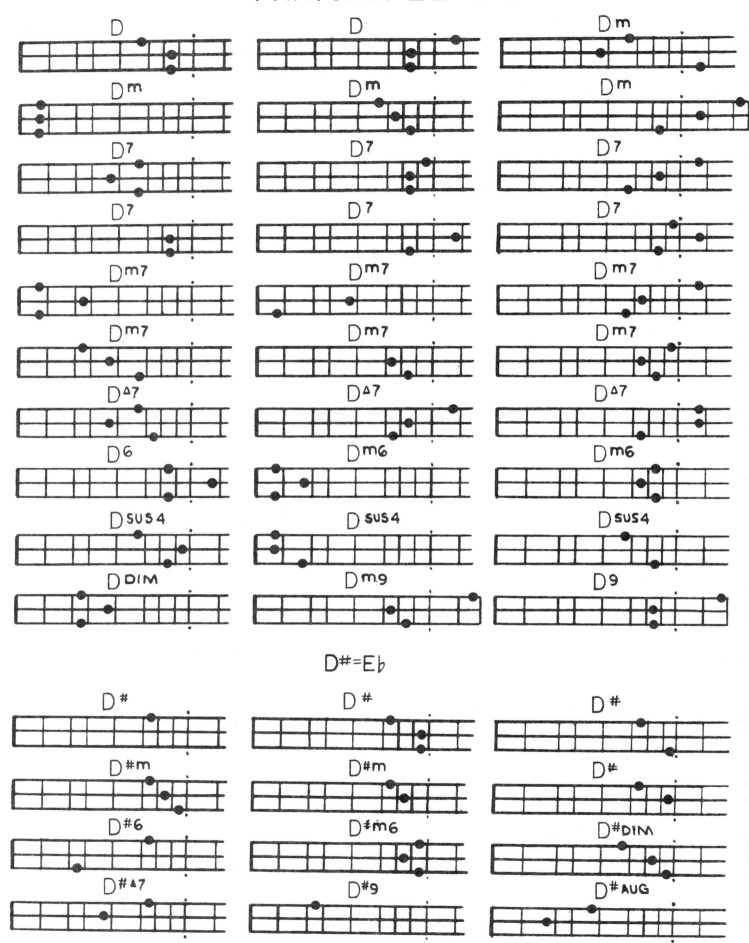

PHRYGIAN E♭E♭-G-C

PHRYGIAN E♭-E♭-G-C

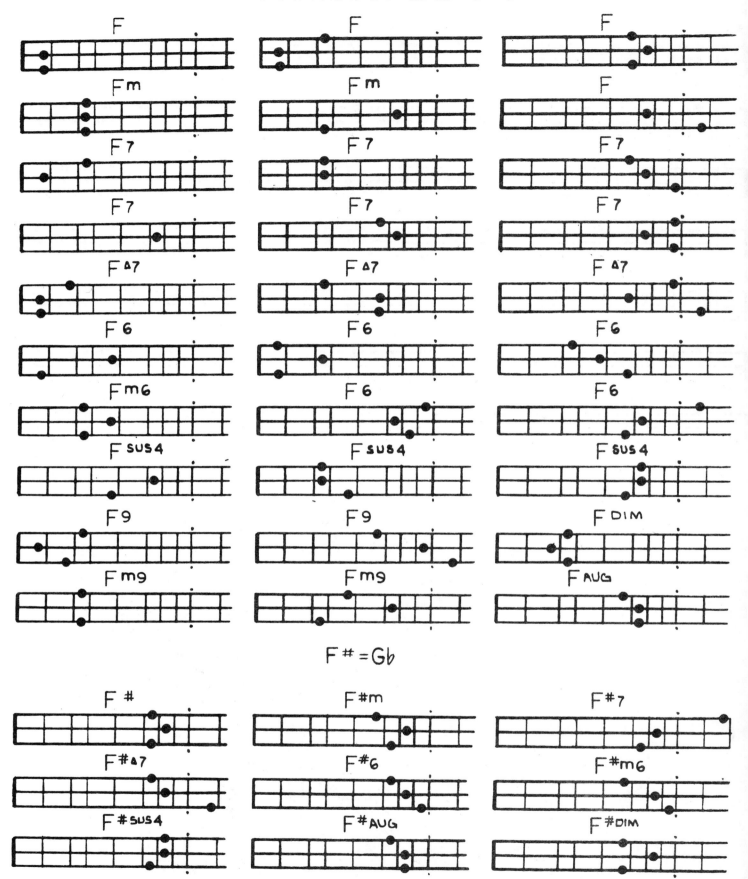

F# = G♭

PHRYGIAN E♭E♭ - G - C

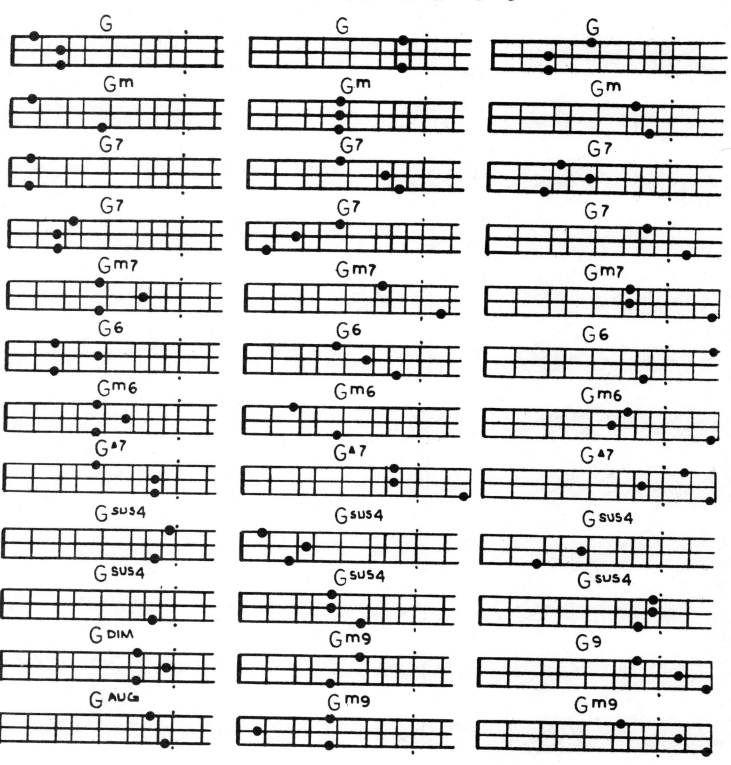

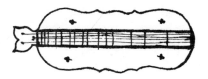